*Publishing: Digitized
and Personalized*

Publishing:
Digitized and Personalized

Anthology Series

Jeremy Allmendinger
Jessica Demarest
Sarah Frazier
Kristen Orlando
Tristan Lozuaway-McComsey
Teagan Bokanovich
Tyler da Silva
Erin Nilssen
Colleen M. Lloyd
Alexandria J. Allen
B.H. Pitt
Andrea Drag
Kara Joyce
Taylor Covington
Zack Miller

Managing Editor: Colleen Rooney
Editor: Kiera Hufford

"Huffington's Oscar" by Jeremy Allmendinger
"4 Innovative Ways to Use Digital Printing for Personalized Publishing" by Jessica Demarest
"Don't Fear Flipboard" by Sarah Frazier
"Stalkertising: Creepy is the New Normal" by Kristin Orlando
"Open Access: Unleashing Education" by Tristan Lozuaway-McComsey
"Photography Books" by Teagan Bokanovich
"The State of Multimedia E-books" by Tyler da Silva
"Why Your Magazine Needs an Animated Title" by Erin Nilssen
"The Debate Between Traditional and Non-Traditional Publishing" by Colleen M. Lloyd
"Packaging the Author" by Alexandria J. Allen
"Going Public: A Look into Online Publishers" by B.H. Pitt
"Can an Author Self-Publish Completely by Him/Herself?" by Andrea Drag
"A Funny Thing Happened When I Joined a Forum" by Kara Joyce
"Step 1: Crowdfund. Step 2: ??? Step 3: Profit." by Taylor Covington
"The Future of Blogging and the Broken Internet Sales Model" by Zack Miller

i

Publishing: Digitized and Personalized
Copyright © by Colleen Rooney

This work was supported by Champlain College Publishing Initiative. Champlain Publishing has not undertaken any independent review or assessment of the quality, accuracy, completeness, currentness, or other aspects of the content and any views or opinions expressed in this book are the views and opinions of the authors and do not necessarily represent those of Champlain Publishing, Champlain College, or its employees, trustees or representatives. The authors alone are solely responsible for the content of the book and bare all responsibility for claims arising from the publication of the book.

Printed in the United States of America

ISBN: 978-0-692-82246-3
First Edition: December 2016

For more information on the Champlain College Publishing Initiative,
visit publishing.champlain.edu.

Cover and interior design and layout by Emma Reed

Table of Contents

Section One: Digital Content

Section Two: Non-Traditional Books

Section Three: Self Publishing

Section Four: The Wide World of the Web

Foreword

As every writer knows, there are many ways to share your voice. The world of writing is fluid, vast, and forever changing. Who had heard of bloggers just ten or fifteen years ago? What options were available to get yourself published besides getting lucky with a publishing house? Now, there are so many options available to writers in so many forms, each changing all the time.

Self-publishing, crowdfunding, digital media—all of this and more has been explored by students at Champlain College in Burlington, VT, as they work to share their voice in the world of writing, in all its many forms. This book serves as a way to share ideas written by students in various publishing classes about different ways to present yourself as a writer to the world.

So go, young grasshoppers! Self-publish! Put your fundraiser on Kickstarter! Create your own e-book! Never stop writing. And never stop learning.

Colleen Rooney, Editor
Champlain Alumna
2016

Huffington's Oscar

By Jeremy Allmendinger

We've got a lot of people to thank.

The world of online publishing and small-press operations is exploding. Thousands of blogs fire up every day. Increasingly, hopeful authors have turned to local publishers to press their words to the page. Traditional publishing houses can afford far fewer risks than before. Most journalists no longer work for the Times or the Post. They cancelled their subscriptions in favor of online citizen newswriting. And they work for free.

The rapid shift in traditional publishing is so strong that the storied halls of the ancient houses in Boston, New York, and Chicago shake beneath the feet of a thousand scrambling editors all trying to keep up. Houses responsible for Vonnegut, Hemingway, and Fitzgerald—long in control of what the world reads—now fight for their place on the front lines. Men and women with forty years in the field are, for the first time, less desirable than bright-eyed young graduates. Senior employees lose their jobs to someone half their age, kicked out for being too experienced. And we've got a lot of people to thank.

This change is hated. This change is loved. It's cursed and praised and trivialized and exaggerated. Your ninety-year-old neighbor may have never heard of Twitter or Facebook, but he has more than a few words to say about the decline of print. It is one of the most well-known dinner party discussions and boardroom arguments of our time. Teachers, children, hermits, athletes, the tie salesman at Macy's, and Uncle Steve all have an opinion. And we've got a lot of people to thank.

People much more qualified than I have written extensively about the rise of digital, the fall of print, the collapse of digital, and the sudden nostalgia of print. They've claimed that books are dead and the Web is dead and used the same eulogy both times. Headlines crowning paper victorious lead to articles declaring online content the King. The intelligent, educated authors of this genre of click-bait have never had firmer convictions, and they've never been more willing to abandon them for a better-selling title.

I will leave those articles to the professionals.

Beyond the BuzzFeeds and Gawkers of the world are actual, scholarly pieces detailing the power struggle and convergence of print and digital. They discuss the future of the publishing industry, the importance of social media, and the effects of both on consumers. I'm not touching that either. I'm writing a thank-you note.

Everyone talks about where we're headed, but few mention the stops along the way. If Arianna Huffington is the movie star accepting an Oscar, who does she thank in her speech? Here is a thank-you note to the original belligerents in the media war.

1. The Phoenicians

Say what you will about these seafaring salesmen, they made some damn good letters. The Phoenician script might be the first widespread alphabetic system, and is certainly one of the most influential. Any fifth grader could tell you that our Roman alphabet comes from these ancient letters; however, Greek, Arabic, many Indian and East Asian languages, and a variety of ancient tongues also owe their written origins to the 22 ancient scribbles that at least three conspiracy theorists probably attribute to aliens.

Phoenician script owes its own backstory to Egyptian hieroglyphs. The letters, which could change appearance depending on who was writing and where, are much simplified versions of the image-based script of the pharaohs. Excluding Chinese, Japanese, and Korean, the vast majority of modern communication relies on alphabets derived from this one ancient alphabet.

Thanks, Phoenicians, for trading words along with wine and forever changing the written world.

2. Johannes Gutenberg

Johannes Gutenberg is best known for being the subject of three out of five middle school essays. Secondarily, he was the inventor of the European printing press. Gutenberg is low-hanging fruit for any article about publishing, but it's hard to overstate his significance.

Before Johnny Goot fell into the historic record, books were painstakingly handmade pieces of art. They were available only to the clergy and the very rich; thus, only the clergy and the very rich had reason to be literate. Once our bearded buddy swooped in with his printing machine, books were suddenly affordable, and gradually the unwashed masses learned their letters.

This sudden access to written knowledge toppled the information monopoly long held by the Church and ruling classes. In many ways, the printing press was a primordial digital revolution—taking the power of information from the hands of a few and giving it to the public. As blogs, image sharing, and Facebook have chipped away at the power of traditional press, Gutenberg's invention turned the informed minority upside down. For the first time in centuries, and possibly more so than ever before, ignorance was no longer excusable.

Thanks, Gutenberg, for turning information into a publicly held commodity.

3. Allen Lane

We're jumping ahead a bit to Allen Lane, chairman of U.K. publisher The Bodley Head. In the 1930s, they were simultaneously a respected institution and on the verge of financial disaster. The Depression hit them hard and, like other publishers, they were struggling to stay in the black. Heads turned to Chairman Lane, who had inherited the job from his uncle.

According to legend, Lane was on his way home from a disappointing visit with Agatha Christie in which no one was murdered. He searched the train station for some quality reading material, but could only find the trashy "penny dreadfuls"—cheap serial literature—bored housewives claimed not to read. Why, he thought, could upstanding literature not also appear in paperback?

Lane pitched the idea to The Bodley Head. They turned him down, worried about investing in a brand new venture when their own future was so uncertain. Using his personal finances, Lane founded Penguin Books with his two brothers. They priced their books to match a pack of cigarettes, making them popular with people who wanted to quit smoking but did not feel like recalculating their monthly budget.

Penguin Books was unique in several ways. First, they were not originally marketed to bookstores. Lane wanted his books at newsstands and pharmacies (Woolworth's was an early distributor). Second, the design of the book focused on the brand, not the author. The covers were incredibly simple and color-coded by genre. A penguin graced the front of each copy.

Lane's venture was enormously successful. Each book had to sell 17,000 copies before making a profit. After just one year, Penguin had sold more than 3 million. They continue to be a dominant force in publishing, while The Bodley Head name now exists only as intellectual property. Lane had launched a profitable product in the midst of a depression, reversed the reputation of the paperback, and founded a major publishing company when nobody else would even invest. Paperback books have been a mainstay of publishers for decades. Lane paved that road.

But wait. Struggling publishers? Financial collapses? Taking an old industry in a bold new direction? Sounds a lot like what we're seeing now. Every publisher—especially former juggernauts like Random House and Pearson—is desperately searching for the next big thing. They know the meaning of words like "blog" and "social media," but they don't know the application. Without an Allen Lane on staff, the Big Four now watch as small, savvy operations take their business. Years of experience are now a hindrance, and veterans of publishing lose their jobs to college grads who think a punch card gets them a free drink with ten purchases.

Thanks, Allen Lane, for softening our covers and our hearts.

4. Justin Hall, Jorn Barger, and Other Pioneer Bloggers

Blogging is great. It's just really great. Sure, there are a lot of god-awful, snail-spit blogs. Yeah, the sites are one of the leading distributers of misinformation on the Web. Sure, some of them are designed using a color scheme that looks like an explosion at the Crayola factory, or vomit more moving images than a feature-length film. We're just going to ignore those.

The blogs that have actually had an impact have really had an impact. From live commentary on the September 11th attacks to reports from Middle-East war zones, weblogs help people around the world stay connected and informed. We owe the success of this hugely influential genre of website to a very small number of early adopters, chief among them Justin Hall.

Justin Hall's site, Justin's Links from the Underground, celebrated its 20th anniversary in 2014. The site's famously exhibitionist writing style led other bloggers to write about their personal lives as well. Weblogs changed from a library of links to the online diary style so closely tied to them today. Hall is generally regarded as the "founding father of personal blogging."

At first glance, Jorn Barger is a beard wearing a man's face. He looks like he could fit an industrial farm and processing center in his facial hair, and may very well have once stood outside a New York City bank yelling about that one time he saw Jesus pushing Gandhi on a swing while Castro personally murdered JFK. But damn if he isn't a visionary.

Barger has been active online pretty much since the first site went live. He coined the term "weblog" and continues to write his own, Robot Wisdom, while simultaneously holding absolutely no long-term employment—a fact he is evidently rather proud of. A digital transparency advocate and acknowledged "online legend," Barger also writes extensively about the "connection between artificial intelligence and the masterworks of James Joyce." Do with that information what you will.

Dave Winer of Scripting News, Scott Rosenberg of www.salon.com, and other pioneer bloggers led the way to the personalized, digitized revolution we now call the blogosphere. Love it or hate it, blogs are here to stay. Even the shitty ones.

Thanks, pioneer bloggers, for giving idiots and intellectuals alike a soapbox, and audience, and 15 minutes of fame.

5. Nicholas Carr and Yochai Benkler

Back in 2006, Nicholas Carr commented on a blog post by Harvard professor Yochai Benkler. Carr—known for his book The Shallows: What the Internet Is Doing to Our Brains and the 2008 article "Is Google Making Us Stupid?"—disagreed with Benkler's theory that the Internet of 2006 was moving towards peer-produced content. Rather, he thought the price-incentivized system used by traditional news media would emerge victorious. The dispute led to the Carr-Benkler wager: If, by 2011, the dominant sites relied on voluntary, peer-produced content, Carr would buy Benkler dinner. If those sites still paid writers for material, Benkler would pick up the check.

In 2011, Carr claimed he had definitively won. Benkler disagreed. Both knew from the start that they would not get a black-and-white answer. Both systems would still co-exist. But it seems even their criteria for which was the dominant system was cause for debate. Benkler cited Facebook, Twitter, YouTube, and Wikipedia as some of the most visited sites in the world. None of these pay users for content creation. Carr acknowledged this, but added that the most popular pages on Facebook and the most viewed videos on YouTube were all commercial productions. Popular opinion seems to be with Yochai Benkler. To this day, neither has admitted defeat.

Publishing houses aren't the only ones who don't fully understand the Web. Even the experts can't agree.

Thanks, Yochai Benkler and Nicholas Carr, for your delightfully passive-aggressive lover's spat that continues to highlight the uncertainty of online trends.

So lastly… We have a lot of people to thank. This list barely scratches the surface. The Web is a constantly evolving, never-slowing, organic lifeform that everyone knows and nobody understands. Within minutes, this small, simple list could appear on BuzzFeed with the title "5 Print-Murdering Maniacs You Didn't Know You Secretly Wanted to Thank and Also We Miss the 90s."

Thanks, print-murdering maniacs, for making that possible.

Section One

Digital Content

4 Innovative Ways to Use Digital Printing for Personalized Publishing

Jessica Demarest

You're shopping for a new car, and you know exactly what you're looking for: a red coupe with black leather seats, premium speakers, and a sunroof. In today's world of mass customization? No problem.

Henry Ford's assembly line is old news, and most products manufactured today are highly customizable, allowing consumers to choose colors and features to personalize their purchases. It's called mass customization, and it's made its way into just about every industry there is, including book publishing.

First, let's cover some background information. This phenomenon wouldn't be possible if not for the rise of digital printing. Offset may be the current standard, but digital printers are rapidly taking over. More and more publishers are printing shorter book runs to avoid waste, and the rise of self-publishing has caused the popularity of print-on-demand to skyrocket. Unless you're printing thousands of copies of books, it just doesn't make sense to print using offset anymore.

And if these advantages aren't convincing enough, digital printing has one more thing going for it offset just can't compete with: variable data printing (VDP). You see, when you print on a digital printer, you upload a file of what you're printing to a computer. The computer then reads it and prints it off. This means there's no transferring an inked image from a plate to rubber and then onto the paper itself.

Instead, digital printers use a dry ink and electrostatically charged plate cylinders to either attract or repel the ink from the paper. Unlike offset printing, VDP plates can be recharged with a new image on every rotation, allowing printers to change certain elements of the file, such as text, images, or colors, each time they print off a copy.

Variable data printing is the driving force behind personalization in book publishing. Some companies have already begun to take advantage of VDP by developing personalized marketing campaigns. Have you ever gotten a brochure or flyer with your name incorporated into the design? When I was a senior in high school, in the process of applying to colleges, I received countless postcards from a bunch of different schools, all proclaiming, "Jessica, picture yourself at Lyon College!" or "Jessica, are you ready to start building your future?"

Phil Gramling, a sales representative at Queen City Printers in Burlington, VT, filled me in on all kinds of ways marketers have been using variable data printing. Basically, it's all about the data. Once you have the data, the digital printing machines allow you to personalize pretty much whatever you want. There's a lot more pre-press work involved in VDP than there is for printing a standardized copy, so it will probably be a little more expensive. Exact estimates are hard to come by because of the very nature of VDP; everything is personalized and unique, which makes it hard for printing companies to hand out a standardized price list. But I can tell you that the difference in pricing is minimal, and primarily a result of extra pre-press time. For more exact numbers, get in touch with a printer that houses a digital press and request a custom quote. I recommend getting multiple numbers, that way you know you have the best deal. But even if it is more than offset printing, results prove that VDP is worth a slightly higher price tag.

Take veterinary clinics, for example. They have all kinds of data on their clients, particularly on what type of animal each person owns. By taking these records and doing a little nifty pre-press formatting, a printer can then print out personalized advertisement materials for each client. So if you own a cat, a flyer with a picture of a cat on it will show up in your mailbox. The same goes for dogs, parrots, iguanas—whatever!

Variable data printing is a great marketing strategy; people love to feel special. Have you seen the Coca-Cola™ bottles with names on them? That's variable data printing at work. Appealing directly to consumers using these types of marketing strategies increases sales and improves customer relations.

But personalization doesn't have to stop with marketing. In fact, there are plenty of ways publishers and other companies can utilize digital printing capabilities. Let's explore a few different projects book publishers could undertake thanks to variable data printing:

1. Make it Your Own: Multiple Cover Options

Maybe you have a favorite character or there's one particular theme in a book that really just sells it for you. That, you're thinking. That's why I love this book! Variable data printing could make it possible for publishers to publish the same book with multiple different covers.

Say you've got a book about travel, food, and love. You know some of your readers love it for the adventure, so they're more likely to want a copy that somehow displays the travel elements of the story. Someone in it for the romance, though, might prefer a cover image featuring the main couple in the story. With variable data printing, you could print multiple copies of the same book, each catering to a different section of your audience. And who knows, it might just increase sales, because if you're a reader like me, you probably won't be able to choose and you'll end up buying them all.

2. Just for You: Personalized Dust Covers

Now, I'll be the first to tell you what a huge fan of bookstores I am, but that doesn't change the fact that more and more people are shopping online. That means they're ordering books online, too. So, wouldn't it be neat if those books were personalized? Think about how many people go out and purchase nice, hardcover copies of their favorite books to display proudly on their bookshelves or gift to a special friend or relative. With variable data printing, publishers could offer a personalized dust cover with the reader's name printed on it. Consumers would gladly pay a few extra dollars to feel personally connected to the book, and I'd bet they'd all look so nice lined up on your shelf!

3. Have it Your Way: Choose Your Own Ending!

Did you ever read one of those choose-your-own-adventure novels as a kid? I know I did. Imagine if you could do that with other books, too. When Phil and I were talking, he mentioned this great idea about readers being able to choose their own endings for a novel. It would go something like this: the author would write the book and then, at a certain point near the end, she would start veering off into different directions. She'd have, let's say, three different endings. Maybe one would be a sad ending, one would be a happy ending, and the last one might be somewhere in between. As a reader, when you're ordering your copy of the book, you can decide where you want it to go.

As long as the author wrote up the content, it would be pretty easy to run the book in three different ways on a digital printer. Something like this would be really neat in a book series—you'd have a whole web of different plot lines branching off in different directions. You could simply make your choices and read straight through, or you could try them all and decide which story you like best.

4. Be a Star: Customized Novels

Wouldn't you love to star in your very own novel? It's not an impossible concept. In fact, several online companies have been providing this service for years. Essentially, a writer writes a book, and then the customer provides the writer with certain personal details to be inserted into the story. Currently, this type of service has been primarily used for children's books and romance novels. Kids are encouraged to read when they're directly involved in the story, and adults can give their significant others heartfelt, personalized gifts. And who knows, maybe you just want to read a story in which you're the hero, so you order one for yourself! There are all kinds of possibilities for growth in the future.

My imagination could run wild with ideas, but these are four of the most interesting ways I think variable data printing might present itself in the future. Sure, right now people are just thinking about marketing strategies, but the digital press can offer a lot more than that. There are all kinds of innovative new ways for book publishers to connect with their readers. The more traditional, standard novel form definitely isn't going to fall by the wayside, but it's safe to say that personalized books could easily start accounting for a much bigger piece of the publishing pie in the near future.

Don't Fear Flipboard

Sarah Frazier

The idea of "new" often reads as "convenient," and in our tech-heavy society "new" also means consolidation, time-saving, and customization. "New" knows what you want. It must prove clever enough to gain public approval and follow through on market fails, then understand how to improve them. Publishing is in desperate need of "new." The evolutions of portable devices such as smartphones and tablets have changed the way we think about not only "new" but "news." Enter the social aggregator; enter Flipboard.

Flipboard is a free app for the Android, iPhone, and iPad, and is called a social aggregator. As an aggregator, it connects feeds from Facebook, Twitter, you name it, into one convenient location in a beautiful magazine layout. It consolidates various sources of interest from film, news, TV, celebrity gossip, tech, science, food, design, print publications, etc. Blogs, acclaimed news sources, obscure news sources, and areas of pondering wonders you thought were buried deep within the Web all come together in this unique specimen of a customized information feed. Not only can you read your favorite magazines, newspapers, and blogs, but Flipboard allows you to create your own customized, online magazine.

Flipboard, and social aggregators like it such as Feedly, offer a new hope for publishers struggling to attract consistent and loyal readership in the digital age. Digital strategist and author Rahaf Harfoush published an article addressing just that—a solution for publishing through the Flipboard medium. In her article, "Flipboard and the Reading Revolution," Harfoush says many publishers, including magazine publishers, are stuck in paid-for clunky online applications that she describes as "glorified PDFs." She says that "by not simply converting their content and putting it online, publishers are missing out on an opportunity to engage with readers on two levels"—multimedia experience and social interaction. Harfoursh sees the potential Flipboard is providing readers and publishers: "Flipboard is a positive step towards the next iteration of publishing. Let's hope others follow to provide readers with a beautifully designed and easy-to-use customized reading experience."

Consumers are all about convenience these days, and publishing is having a hard time keeping up with this concept. Many argue that there are already apps available from these sources online and in the app stores. This is true, but consumers are interested in saving time and customization, and Flipboard allows more than just what these individual sources can provide. It is the ultimate middle man—a model of what modern publishing is heading towards.

But what is the function of that model? How is it lucrative? And how can not only big publishers, but self-publishers get on the bandwagon? Flipboard currently has 85 million users worldwide, but its operational idea isn't anything new to most in the publishing world—it's advertising. Yes, advertising brings in the bank. According to an article by Media Post, "Flipboard CEO Explains How Brand Is Monetizing Users," there are more than 3.5 million customized titles created for the public on Flipboard, and it's growing.

The article goes on to explain that paid advertising only appears in formal publishing partners like that of Vanity Fair; however, Flipboard offers publishers full-page ads, "…on a share-of-mind basis of up to 25 percent for a given publication in the app, or four advertisers per publication. In effect, users see ads about every ten pages overall," according to CEO Mike McCue. Publishers can sell those ads directly or through Flipboard. Brands with customized magazines are increasingly using these ads to drive traffic to their Flipboard titles, much as many advertisers on Facebook try to steer users toward their brand pages.

There is also something psychologically soothing to the consumer on Flipboard when they don't have to see ads juxtaposed with the articles they're trying to read. Instead, the full-page ads are witnessed only when readers flip the pages. According to McCue, due to the magazine experience of Flipboard, these full-page ads can sell for the equivalent of that to print ads. This, McCue says, allows for a content monetization of ten – one-hundred times that of banner ads normally seen on websites and apps.

Typical watch time for Flipboard averages 15 minutes per use, with brand magazines witnessing 20 – 40 pages flipped per session. Publishers may worry about brand or ad reception (aka strength of the brand), but a study done by Nielsen, a global information and market research company, found that "comparing brand metrics for advertising in the app with the same ad content in other media showed it had higher brand recall and favorability—80 percent and 70 percent respectively—than on TV, Web, and radio." As readers, we couldn't care less about ad statistics, but this is fantastic news for those marketers, publishers, and advertisers trying to survive in the ever-changing publication market.

In a recent Digital Pivot post entitled "Three Reasons Why Flipboard is Not Just Another Pretty Face," Lisa Thorell explains that it's the potential of the platform that has many in the tech world excited. Speaking on Flipboard's potential ad revenue, the semantic indexing capabilities that allow for consumer/user customization "across their social network based around any ad hoc topic of choice," she explains how this puts Flipboard in an interesting position: "It is, in fact, this advanced technological competence that will distinguish Flipboard's position in the ad-value chain, much as Google became an 'intermediary' with Google AdWords."

The growth of ad and revenue expectations aren't the only thing that Thorell and others mark as extraordinary, but also the potential learning capabilities, similar to Netflix, that could spring from the Flipboard medium. Much like Netflix customizes to your viewing pleasure, Flipboard is well on its way to possibly the same function with your reading. While this is still in works, it is a revolutionary concept in the publishing platform.

Flipboard recently raised $50 million, and has gained $111 million to date. Flipboard plans to use this funding for its expansion: hiring people to sell ads, acquiring more engineering staff, and generally growing their offices in New York and Beijing. Needless to say, they aren't slowing down.

Flipboard users can expect a comprehensive, functional platform. I personally use it for most of my own reading, an average of more than an hour a day.

If I want to save articles I've read for later, I simply add them to my own created magazine aggregator, Illuminated Balloons. Users can create their own magazine aggregators. Up in the corner of each article is a plus sign, which allows you to keep articles you wish to save for later. Other users may then search through your individualized collection of content and subscribe. Many have created genre-specific collectives that make it easier for fans of certain topics (surfing, Game of Thrones, etc.) to find their areas of interest.

Flipboard is a publishing platform that has changed the way we think about reading, finding, and viewing our news and favorite editorials. It plays to our notions of digitally shared content and instant gratification. It's a treat for users and a solution for publishers.

Stalkertising:
Creepy is the New Normal
Kristen Orlando

Borders was my bookstore. I loved the atmosphere, selection, and that the price stickers peeled off without fuss. I remember perusing the aisles and finding what I wanted, or maybe one or seven books I didn't even know existed. Now, I don't have time for bookstores (Borders, rest in peace), but I still want to read whenever I can. And now my book decisions are made for me.

I read The Fault in Our Stars, liked it on Amazon, and had instant recommendations for what I should read next or what other people also bought. I've purchased three books as a result. My favorite YouTube cat is Lil Bub—I watch the videos and follow the owner on social media—so when I logged into Amazon and was offered a pre-order of Bub's book, I was on my way to confirming payment before I even realized what was happening.

What was happening?

Amazon was "stalkertising" me. This isn't ordinary advertising anymore. Book publishers aren't wasting time and money getting their products to vast groups of possible readers—they're pulling them in one by one. Currently, there is nothing more important than keeping an existing/creating a new fan base, and publishers are not going to do this if they don't individualize advertising.

There's a push to have an online brand/presence for publishers, authors, and just about anybody; however, it is no longer enough. If any of these groups intend on staying afloat in the dwindling attention spans of readers, they need to use the recent, possibly creepy, marketing trend.

It's going to come down to verticalization: audience-centric marketing that helps publishers broaden their fan base and, in turn, success. This means several things: 1) Marketing is no longer relying on getting the message out—it is gaining the interest and trust of consumers; 2) Marketing accommodates the individual/personal needs of every customer; 3) Marketing agents can never again depend on customers finding them—they have to make the first move.

Not only does this matter to publishing, but it could determine its future success and longevity.

Mike Shatzkin, founder and CEO of The Idea Logical Company, examines verticalization and how it is going to change the way publishers must market their books, authors, and selves. He says: "It didn't used to matter to publishers if they had the 'next book' for the person who bought the last book. But it surely does when you've spent good marketing money and effort to find and reach that person, and when you can often stay in touch with them in a cost-free (or at least very low-cost) way going forward."

I bring up Shatzkin here because he is a publishing leader and continues to push publishing into the future. But what about examples of verticalization that aren't funded or driven by "big wigs" like Shatzkin or Amazon or Google? We know about them. We expect them to find new ways to "stalkertise" us because they always do. (My Google recommends purple accessories, gluten and dairy free food products, and a constant supply of puppy videos without me ever asking. Do you think I told Google my favorite color was purple?)

Here are some smaller examples of what's going on in the publishing world's marketing that speaks to verticalization, demonstrates how crucial being creepy is, and makes me buy more books.

1. Cristin O'Keefe Aptowitz

Cristin is backed by Write Bloody Publishing, where she has published six books of poetry. What makes Write Bloody Publishing a great example is how they allow Cristin to market and reach out to individual fans. As a fan of Cristin, you are already connected with her personally on Facebook, Twitter, and through the Bowery Poetry Club. Through these connections, fans are offered individual perks like first views on new videos, access to more poetry, and, most recently, a very individualized advertising of her newest book.

Cristin's sixth book came out in October 2013. For a certain number of days before its release, she posted a poem from past books or a few sneak peeks at the new one on her Facebook page. So what? Well, here's what that did: every single day, I saw a post with a link to a poem by one of my favorite poets with the Write Bloody Publishing name thrown in on my personal Facebook page. If Cristin had posted these on her blog, website, or through Write Bloody Publishing, I wouldn't have seen them.

This is inventive marketing because 1) it wasn't just one Facebook post that I would read, think about, and then move on from because it happened daily; 2) I saw it every time because it showed up somewhere I already visit online every day; and 3) it made me care about her project because she was personally advocating for herself and giving me daily poems to read. Usually, if someone is trying to get me to buy something when I'm busy looking at pictures of my two-year-old niece apple picking or posting a video of my golden retriever opening a birthday present, I'm not going to be happy; however, I chose to be connected with Cristin on Facebook and I chose to allow her posts to show up on my newsfeed. Not only was I not bothered, but I'm going to buy the book (and I already know like it).

2. John Green

You heard it from me: John Green is going to control the Internet and his following is going to help him control the world (probably). John has written five books (he uses Dutton books, a division of Penguin) and is the co-founder of Vlogbrothers, Brotherhood 2.0. If this sounds unfamiliar to you, it's time for a YouTube search.

John Green had been busy publishing four books and vlogging with his brother Hank creating the Nerdfighter culture and an immense following of fans. When it came time for his fifth, The Fault in Our Stars, to be published in 2012, John spent 2011 getting the message out to his fans. With the help of Dutton publishers, however, he did much more.

John announced, in a video on YouTube, that he would autograph the entire first printing of the book if the fans would like it. They liked it. They liked it and they pre-ordered so many books that the first printing got pushed up to 150,000 books instead of its first estimation, and the release date of the book got pushed to January. Signing 150,000 books became a fan spectacle overnight. John made a progress thermometer, signed books during some videos, and started customizing them based on individual fan demand.

In doing this, every book became an individualized book. The Fault in Our Stars is not just a book, it's my book. (I have a green "J-scribble" signature.) I had been meaning to read John's books for a while since becoming a Nerdfighter and figured I would eventually get to all of them. Being a part of watching John sign 150,000 books, read excerpts when Dutton permitted it, and see all the fan art and support before the book was even in warehouses convinced me that I needed to start reading John Green immediately—starting with The Fault in Our Stars and preordering a signed copy.

I wasn't the only fan who felt this connection—The Fault in Our Stars sold out of preorders and has already been reprinted enough that it hit the one million copies printed mark before it's publishing anniversary in January 2013. This happened because 1) The Fault in Our Stars is a great book (awarded the best young adult book in 2012); 2) John is incredibly accessible and aware of each and every one of his fans; and 3) readers felt connected to this book before it was even published.

Let's end with a quick look back to "stalkertising" and what we should expect from publishing. You don't have to go to a bookstore to look for what you might like to read next (although, please do once in a while so they don't all meet their sad, dramatic deaths). You are contacted by authors and publishers through your personal websites, emails, etc. You don't feel pressured into buying books because the advertising is so tailored to you that you'll thank publishers for sending you those recommendations since they're exactly what you didn't know you needed.

Now, books are dedicated to you, written to you, and all around for you in every way possible. It isn't creepy—it's just normal. And you don't have to look for books. They find you.

Open Access:
Unleashing Education
Tristan Lozuaway-McComsey

In 2013, I took a class on short stories. The readings for the class all came from the required textbook, which was, essentially, an anthology of short stories from authors who wrote between the early nineteenth century and just a couple decades ago. As the semester progressed, I became more and more frustrated that I spent a month's worth of utility money on this textbook when all of the material could be found online. What a baboon my teacher is for making us buy the textbook! I thought. Even in my complete ignorance to copyright laws, I was partially right. Some of the short stories we read—"To Build a Fire" (1908) by Jack London, for instance—are now registered as public domain and can be used in the educational realm without repercussion. The professor could have printed it out, brought the copies into class, and distributed them to without endangering his career or bringing liability to the educational establishment.

We also read modern works by authors who are still alive and retain the rights to the works. If you looked hard enough, all of the pieces of literature that we needed to read were online, though they were not there legally and could not be used for educational purposes. This was an issue of public domain under copyright law.

That same year, I had to buy a textbook for a mandatory environmental studies class. We bought a $70 textbook to read two out of fourteen chapters from it over the course of the semester. I threw an internal tantrum that my professor didn't just scan the chapters, post them online, and save us a collective $910. Unfortunately, copying two chapters of the book is over the acceptable fair use amount, which is typically around ten percent (or sometimes rounded off to one chapter).

Though my professor was right not to scan and distribute the chapters to the class, she may still have been able to give us worthwhile text on the same discussion without creating fees or liability. An alternative route would have cost her a few extra hours of research but she could have saved us a nearly four-figure sum collectively by bringing public domain works to class. These would probably be a little outdated but still extremely useful, with a grain of salt and an educated professor to lead discussion. She could have also extracted excerpts from academic journals, essays, a chapter from a book, or even entire poems (up to 250 words) to aid the educational process on a daily basis. This accessibility available to professors and students, due to the Internet, is enabling a lot of works to be used in the classroom legally; however, establishments like Georgia State University prove how important it is to watch where you click.

Georgia State found themselves in court with three publishing companies because a professor distributed a packet to his students that contained copyrighted material that he neglected to cut into fair use size. The Chronicle of Higher Education reported that "Judge Orinda D. Evans ruled that Georgia State had violated copyright with the online course reserves, known as 'e-reserves,' in only five of 99 instances alleged by the plaintiffs. The publishers appealed that ruling."

The appeal was made so that the court would take a closer look at the United States copyright and fair use factors. The factors to be considered are:

- the purpose and character of your use
- the nature of the copyrighted work
- the amount and substantiality of the portion taken
- the effect of the use upon the potential market

The publishers deemed the content used by Georgia State to be in conflict with the third factor because of the magnitude of the articles used. They wrote: "The District Court should have analyzed each instance of alleged copying individually, considering the quantity and quality of the material taken—whether the material taken constituted the heart of the work—and whether that taking was excessive in light of the educational purpose of the use." You can start to see how easily dispute could arise from copyrighted material because the basis of whether or not you can use it depends on the ability to identify "the heart of the work."

This case began a few years ago and, after closing in heavy favor of the University, it was reopened and is now leaning more towards the publishers after going through a federal court. The case may not close for some more time as the guidelines of fair use continue to teeter. Though we may never see a definitive fair use law that makes copyright cases easy to decide, there is an alternative that is creating some motion across the pond (and a little bit in the United States as well). It is called "open access" and it may well be the future of free international higher education.

Open access has one main priority: increase access to academic research. The roots of open access are hazy and debatable, though one of the first bold signs of it can be traced to India in 1909 to one of the world's most recognizable names: Mahatma Gandhi. Gandhi's Hind Swaraj is printed with the words "No Rights Reserved" on the inside cover. It was a stance taken to promote the freedom of India from both physical and intellectual restraints. At that point in time (more so than now), open access identified with communist ideals because it would cost the public to print the copies that needed to be distributed. Open access made less sense purely because creation and distribution would cost governments, and thus the people, a pretty penny. This somewhat dilutes the essence of open access.

With the creation and evolution of the Internet, open access took on its current and most refined form. A few companies, including National Academies Press who started publishing open access documents on the Internet as early as 1994, have taken the initiative to share digital academic research without charge. One distinction that needs to be made—and open access publishing houses, make note of this—is that open access does not mean the work is free to edit or republish.

Global Open Access Portal (GOAP) is an organization working between the United States, a few European countries, and Colombia to gain open access education for their peoples. The dream is to gather all the scientific research available and convert it to open access information. GOAP believes that free research not only assists those in the first world countries but enables those in third world countries to make something for themselves and contribute to global research. Currently, teachers are using the open domain documents, and plenty of fair use excerpts, to enhance the education of pupils, but the future may lie in the death of copyright.

The future of education could very well be intertwined with, and possibly even dependent on, open access education. It allows educational facilities, scientific researchers, engineers, and all makes of intellectuals to enhance their research and quicken the pace in which they are able to produce their own shareable publication. The Internet worked wonders for the scientific community as well as for educational facilities, but open access has been promised by some to be the key that unleashes the Internet to its full capabilities. If open access becomes widely accepted, it could help develop third world countries, hasten medical studies, and change the direction in which the educational realm spins. Imagine when your kids get into a college and you don't have to buy their textbooks. Wouldn't that be nice?

Section Two
Non-Traditional Books

Photography Books
Teagan Bokanovich

When I was growing up in my house, the coffee table was always covered in magazines and photo albums. As I grew older, the table became home to many different photography books. From National Geographic's best images of the year to dog-portrait pages to simple rolling green hills and stark white fields, those books captured my attention better than a TV show ever could. I was always wrapped up in the beauty that lay on the pages before me.

Growing up in the digital age, I started seeing more and more images online, and began putting my own images up as well. Before I knew it, those photo books were piled in a box and hidden on a shelf somewhere in my house.

The digital age, with all its ease and amazing finds, has also brought a lot of worry, especially for the future of print books. With e-books, paper books aren't necessary anymore. Why have a heavy book with 100+ pages when you can have one object that could store thousands of books within it? Since the rise of these e-books, many people have been concerned about the future of print. Newspapers started fading out in lieu of online editions, and many books are now offered in an e-book form before a print version is made available. I wonder, with all of these changes to the written word, what it means for those printed books that I used to lose myself in. Will I only be able to find photo books on an online platform, and only be able to look at gorgeous images through a screen?

Will the future bring with it a world where having an image on print is a thing of the past? Will turning pages become archaic? E.B., an economist journalist who wrote about e-books versus the written form, says: "I was always under the impression that books served a dual purpose: not only do they offer a world to enter, but also they offer an affordable means of escape from the world we're in. What a nice cloak a book can be on the subway or the train, or while sitting at a bar, enjoying the buzz of humanity while absorbed in something else.

"We are so distracted by and engulfed by the technologies we've created, and by the constant barrage of so-called information that comes our way, that more than ever to immerse yourself in an involving book seems socially useful.... The place of stillness that you have to go to write, but also to read seriously, is the point where you can actually make responsible decisions, where you can actually engage productively with an otherwise scary and unmanageable world."

Children's author and child expert, Lisa Guernsey, was in Burlington, VT, in October 2014 for a conference and sat down with WCAX's Gina Bullard for an interview. The interview was about how much screen time children have. The two spoke briefly about e-books and about what is to come in the future. I found it really interesting to learn that e-books aren't the best things for children. Physical books are better for their imagination, well-being, learning comprehension, and their mental development.

"Librarians especially are really grappling with this [e-books vs. paper books], and so are parents. We're seeing so far that there is something different about an e-book, an e-picture book with a child, than a print book, and we need to start being aware of the differences," says Guernsey. If e-books aren't the best for our children, why is there still a debate that they will be replacing print books?

Hayley Lovell, an alumna of Champlain College's Professional Writing program, weighed in on her thoughts about electronic books: "I don't think e-books will ever wipe out print, for a number of reasons, but specifically because hard-copy books are a niche market, and also because e-books are a privilege. You need the technology to access e-books and unfortunately, even though we have made massive strides with that technology, it still is a luxury not everyone can afford.

"Also, when e-books first came out everyone scrambled, claiming that this was the end of print books but that was just under a decade ago and print books are still going strong. But e-books are a unique medium and they allow for a new avenue of publishing. It's an easy way to allow for people to self-publish—a cheap and effective way to self-publish. I personally don't like e-books. I prefer the weight of a book in my hands and pages between my fingers—I will probably end up being one of those people who keeps print alive purely because I love the feeling so much."

The pros for online photo books are swaying many artists to self-publish in these online forums and market themselves. It is much cheaper to produce something in an online format than to create an actual book. Creating a physical book is a large feat. It takes time, money, resources, and decisions (from page sizes to length, glossy versus matte, hardcover versus paperback, and which company to print with). Not to mention that after creating a book, it is highly likely an author or artist will need a publisher in order to get all the necessary and required elements to sell the book. Printing a high-quality, high-resolution book full of color images is quite expensive. Finding the correct resolution for photos and making sure they print to the quality preferred is not easy and can cost an arm and a leg. It's much easier to create a website or online gallery with endless amounts of images, and it's much easier to just put high-resolution images on the web.

A large part of the decision between digital photo books and print books depends on the artist and their preference. It can also depend on money, resources, and the number of images an artist might want to print, but it's ultimately up to the artists. Artists of my generation might prefer a digital version because it is what we grew up with and we can customize the photo book to our liking. Older artists might prefer a physical book because it is what they are used to and it's easier than trying to adapt to the Internet. In my personal opinion, I don't think that print photo books will ever fully be a thing of the past. Some of the bigger, more intense ones might be, but I think companies like National Geographic will always produce books. I also think future artists will prefer the magical moment when their images are on pages of their book in front of them, and the pages are being turned all around the world.

"Scrolls continued to be used for hundreds of years after the codex was developed. Early printed books tried to diminish the shock of the new by looking like handwritten manuscripts, rather as e-books have, to date, aged print," claims The Economist in their October 2014 issue. "Books will evolve online and off, and the definition, of what counts as one will expand; the sense of the book as a fundamental channel of culture, flowing from past to future." It seems that, whether it is a print book or a photo book, they are not yet a thing of the past. While physical photo books might still be in a closet somewhere, it doesn't mean that they aren't still being put out on bookshelves in stores and libraries.

The State of Multimedia E-books

Tyler da Silva

Multimedia e-books are a broad sub-genre of published work. While the loosest definitions mark them as "e-books with pictures," some can feature video, audio, and even interactivity. This format pushes the limits of what a book can be, but their creation can be a mess that few authors or publishers would want to deal with.

To start, let's talk of the benefits of multimedia e-books versus normal e-books. The range of possibilities is endless with e-books and vary wildly from book to book. A multimedia Hamlet can contain video clips of live performances, or of scholars providing commentary. A horror novel can have audible door creaks and footsteps that play on the right pages. Some of the multimedia e-books that exist today use as many features as the medium will allow, while others provide sparse images or videos to supplement their content.

The first example, and likely the most impressive one, is Device 6, a "surreal thriller" that has taken the indie gaming and publishing worlds by storm over the past year, but is not well known to those outside. This iOS exclusive app pushes the limits of what a novel can be, crossing into gaming territory in the process. The story centers on Anna, a woman who wakes up in a castle on an island; the reader is presented with normal text and some ambient music. As Anna approaches windows and interesting objects, images appear alongside the text—images that have a 3-D depth to them and pan as the reader scrolls them past the screen. As she finds new hallways and rooms, the paragraphs change direction and shape to draw a map of the castle she's trapped in. And as she finds puzzles she must solve to unlock new areas (or chapters), the reader is also given the puzzles to solve themselves. Popular game-news site IGN gave the app a score of 9.5 out of 10 in their review, and The Atlantic ran a headline that said it could "revolutionize publishing." The app has also seen commercial success, with 200,000 copies sold in its first six months.

While Device 6 is the creative ideal of what a multimedia e-book could be, it is not ideal technically speaking. The studio behind it, Simogo, built the app in Unity, a cross-platform game engine, along with some other software tools like Maya and Adobe Audition. Unity is an acclaimed and popular software kit, especially among indie game studios, thanks to its cross-platform publishing tools and relaxed licensing terms; however, it was not completely ideal for Device 6. Simogo director Simon Flesser has said that Unity's font rendering was, "to be frank, very poor." While they found a plug-in that fixed this issue for them and, in the end, were happy with Unity, Flesser admits that he would have explored other options if given the time.

The next example of a multimedia e-book, and probably the most well-known one, is the iBook Textbook. While "textbook" is the only official term released for them, these books can be of any type and any subject. They are published and sold by Apple, and must be made using Apple's own iBooks Author. Video, audio, photo galleries, interactive diagrams, and even 3-D objects are supported by the format. Time Magazine has praised them for their possibilities and for iBooks Author's ease of use in their May 2014 issue.

While the possibilities are impressive, the format has three major setbacks. First, iBooks Author is only available on Mac OS X—you'd need a Mac computer (or a "Hackintosh") to create an iBook Textbook. Second, the extra features are only supported in the .ibook file format, which can only be read on Mac OS X or iPad. Finally (and this is the most infamous problem), the .ibook file can only be sold for profit in the iBookstore—and Apple takes a 30 percent cut of the revenue. Overall, the file requires at least a $500 Mac Mini to create, the potential audience is limited right out the gate, and Apple takes nearly a third of the money your work would make. This format is less than ideal for many authors.

Over the last few years, popular e-book formats have added some form of multimedia support. The two most popular formats—ePub and Mobipocket (or AZW, as it's known on the Kindle)—both used the obsolete XHTML web language at their core. In the last four years, however, both formats have been updated to use HTML5 and CSS3, the same languages that almost all modern websites use. This means that any e-books using the ePub3 or AZW3 standard can embed video and audio, and have better text formatting/reflow capabilities. The other popular format, PDF, has supported video, audio, and even interactivity with the introduction of the Rich Media PDF over the last ten years.

Unfortunately, these formats aren't perfect either. The common way of creating e-books (formatting in a word processor and exporting to HTML) doesn't always work for these new formats. Microsoft Word's HTML export feature doesn't generate the proper CSS for AZW3, and the same Time Magazine article that praised iBooks Author

Publishing: Digitized and Personalized

reported that at least one multimedia Kindle book looked like it was "laid out by a fourth grader in a version of Microsoft Word from 1992." Additionally, Rich Media PDFs can only be created in Adobe Acrobat (which costs $20 a month) and can only be read in Adobe Acrobat or Adobe Reader.

The ideal multimedia e-book would run on most devices, yet still support digital rights management software in order to prevent piracy. How interactive they are will depend not only on the device but on the story itself. Device 6 puzzles may not work with a textbook, and a thrilling adventure novel won't be made much more thrilling with 3-D rendered objects. Like with adapting books to movies, a creative eye will be needed to decide what is needed and what is not.

Why Your Magazine
Needs an Animated Title

Erin Nilssen

Visual communication is inescapable in today's society. When you read the logo on your morning espresso or look at billboards on your drive to work you are engaging in a visual message. With advancements in technology, the way we present visual content is no longer limited to the physical realm. Through the use of digital media, such as video, we are redefining what it means to be literate. It no longer just means the ability to read or write, but also the ability to communicate on a wide variety of platforms.

With the development of computer software over the past few decades, animation has become more prevalent. Back in 1963, Ivan Sutherland, the co-founder of Pixar Animation Studios, created the program Sketchpad. This was the first basic animation interface, which opened the door to the possibility of moving images. Since then, Adobe has become the leading name in graphic design software, including the ones used for animation. In 1994, Adobe released their first version of After Effects, followed closely in 1996 by the release of Flash.

Today, these programs are used by a wide variety of industries in order to create animated videos that incorporate both motion graphics and kinetic typography. Large corporations (like Pepsi and Starbucks) have begun to use short animations, integrated with video footage, as television commercials; for example, in 2008, Starbucks used animated type in a commercial promoting the presidential election. The commercial was all text-based, but since the text moved it grabbed the viewer's attention and managed to hold it for longer than static type could. It caused the viewers to engage with what they were seeing rather than just tuning it out. Corporations are also using animations in their websites. Various companies have motion infographics, which provide information and statistics on certain products or on the business in general.

Book publishing is another industry that is beginning to make use of animation. One thing that has become popular among many publishers is to create video-book trailers. Video-book trailers are short—roughly one to three minutes—and aim to get people interested in buying the book. They are directly modeled after movie trailers, using visuals as a way to engage the viewer. According to 3M Corporation and Zabisco (a digital agency) in "19 Reasons You Should Include Visual Content in Your Marketing [Data]," an article on Hubspot by Amanda Sibley, "90% of information transmitted to the brain is visual, and visuals are processed 60,000 [times] faster in the brain than text." Essentially, this means that visuals can be understood and processed in the brain faster than static text. It is also easier to get someone to sit and watch a short video than it is to get them to go out of their way to pick up a book and read the back cover.

Book publishing companies and corporate businesses are both following in the footsteps of the movie industry. The movie industry is one of the largest proprietors of computer-generated animation. Between CGI and animated company logos, the movie industry crushes competitors in the multitude of ways that they are using animation.

One thing that movie companies do differently with motion graphics is create an animated logo and title sequence for their company. Every movie put out by DreamWorks opens with a little boy sitting in a crescent-shaped moon. The little boy always casts a fishing line, but the way this happens is different depending on the movie. Most often, the boy starts out on the moon and the DreamWorks logo fades in. In other versions, the boy floats up to the moon while holding onto balloons, or the moon he sits on molds into the letter D. They have the potential to slightly tweak these animations to make them interesting and new while still maintaining the brand's identity. Pixar also has a similar type of opening sequence to their movies. The name Pixar starts out on the screen and a small desk lamp bounces in and crushes the letter I. It then turns and faces the audience, becoming the letter it crushed. These extremely short title animations help capture the viewers' attention and are extremely memorable.

Now imagine opening a digital magazine on your laptop and seeing the name of the magazine presented in a similar way to the DreamWorks and Pixar logos. That would be much more interesting than opening the magazine to see static type. The types of animations used by movie companies, book publishers, and businesses can be applied to the new digital magazine industry.

Many traditional magazines are beginning to publish in an online format. This allows them to maximize the people who see their product while minimizing the production costs. An online magazine can embed video into the pages rather than just having still images. The use of video footage in a digital format is the gateway to the incorporation of animation. By following the trends of animation, we can see that digital magazines have begun to touch on its foundations, but have not yet made use of its full potential.

After looking on digital magazine hosting sites, such as Joomag and ISSUU, you can clearly see that magazine publishing still remains in a more traditional format. Although video, along with text and images, is being used as content, no magazine that I could find has an animated title sequence.

There are several advantages and disadvantages about having an animated title. One of the main advantages to having a motion graphics introduction is that it is more likely to capture the attention of new viewers and get them interested in flipping through the magazine. Engaging, innovative titles have higher click-through rates. More people will view more pages and stay on them for a longer amount of time because they are now captivated and eager to see what other interactive things the magazine will do.

Another big advantage of an animated title sequence is that it can help establish the mood of the magazine before the reader ever reaches the first page. It can demonstrate the theme of the magazine and nature of the topic. The readers will immediately know if what they are about to read will be funny, serious, creative, or formal. Also, according to Simply Measured (a social analytics platform) in the aforementioned Hubspot article, "Videos are shared 1,200% more times than links and text combined." This means that people are more likely to share an animated title. With more people being able to view and share the magazine title, the more views the whole magazine will receive. The more dynamic the introduction, the more likely it is to be shared and talked about.

Although an animated title is more engaging and can produce a higher click-through rate, it also has its disadvantages. The biggest drawback to animation is that it is time consuming to make. The designer must also have a keen eye for aspects like color and typography. Without this eye for design, the animation can easily become overwhelming. There is a fine line between an animation that works in engaging the viewer and one that just irritates them.

An animated title sequence has the potential to make a huge difference in the success of a magazine. Since traditional magazines are static, the images and type have to work incredibly hard to catch reader's interest. The static nature of the cover puts more pressure on it to quickly grab potential readers. At first glance, it has to make people want to pick it up and continue flipping through the pages. It must be an indicator of what else is in the magazine.

Adding animation to the cover of a magazine also changes its identity. As soon as elements begin moving and interacting with one another, the spirit of the magazine changes. It instantly becomes youthful and more creative. It engages with the interest and visual literacy of younger generations. It also opens the door to slight variations in the animation. Like the DreamWorks title sequence, it can change slightly with every movie or, in this case, issue.

As of right now, the full advantages of animation are not being used in the digital magazine industry. Since animation has only begun to gain momentum in the last few decades, its full potential has not yet been realized. As for digital magazines, the advantages of having an animated title outweigh the disadvantages. In a visual culture like ours, it is important to instantly capture the attention of the audience in dynamic and innovative ways.

Section Three

Self-Publishing

The Debate Between Traditional and Non-Traditional Publishing

Colleen M Lloyd

The debate regarding traditional publishing and non-traditional, indie, or self-publishing often pairs the two categories as opposites, one against the other. While some authors are willing to pay the financial price to see their story widely advertised and on bookshelves, others prefer to take the economical, ecological route down the somewhat unexplored street of non-traditional publishing. It boils down to exactly what you want: to have control over the design, or to let someone else take over; put time and money into marketing, or have it handled by a publishing house; go through the editing process with professionals, or depend largely on your own skills; wait for a publishing offer, or make your own. In actuality, the two are not opposites, merely separate but similar means to an end. The choice to traditionally or self-publish depends on you as an author, and what your publication piece needs to be. In the end, authors can be successful through traditional publishing and non-traditional publishing at the same time—as a hybrid author.

The fact is, these two forms of publishing are not made equally, but the product they produce, if done correctly, is more or less the same. Say success of a publishing project is a ratio of the time spent on the project by the author to the total money made from the project by the author a year after publication. Mathematically, to be the most successful, the book would need to take as little time, but sell as many copies, as possible, no matter the publishing venue, editing process, or marketing power.

By this model, the two systems are even: a book with little work put in by the author and more work put in by marketers and editors could ratio 1:1 for the author—one unit of work by the author yields one unit of the total payout (because some portion goes to paying the editors). A book in which the author performs as marketer/designer/editor means they ratio 4:4—four units of work for four times the payout. It is a common theme: you get what you pay for, you earn what you work for.

Now time management comes into the picture. If the traditional author yielding a unit of one for the payout can duplicate the process three more times in the same amount of time as the author who yields a unit of four, and both books have the same ratio level of success, both authors are successfully the same in terms of money. One author published four books and made $3,000. The other published one book and also made $3,000. Totally fair, right?

But time and money are not the only factors in play. Authors publish for a number of reasons: a chance to tell their story, to prove something to themselves, being a known literary figure, or connecting with an audience, in addition to mere dividends. Considering these factors, and their importance to the author, you can determine which type of publishing will best serve a written work.

Both self-publishing and traditional publishing will make a manuscript into a commodity, but it's time to discuss how they differ. It is difficult to pinpoint the pros and cons of either because there is a wide range of results, and, like anything else, all rules have glaring exceptions.

Say you meet two authors; we'll call them Sam and Rebecca. Sam has written a trendy young adult vampire romance novel. Rebecca has written a memoir about the difficulty of growing up with a parent in the military. Each is working with Stonebrook, a traditional publishing house that knows what sells.

Stonebrook tells Sam to edit out three characters. They choose a cover for the book, the layout, the font. At the last minute, they even change the title. Sam doesn't mind. He wants to hit the literary world like wildfire. He wants to rake in the dough! The book is released a year after Sam signed the contract and it is nowhere close to the original manuscript. Sam wanted fame and glory. Stonebrook did not organize the type of spectacular book tour he had expected, but he rates his publishing experience 8/10.

Stonebrook has similar edits for Rebecca. They tell her to spice up her memoir, add more detail about parts she deemed irrelevant, and choose from two cover designs, both of which she dislikes. Rebecca feels uncomfortably out of control through the entire process. She doesn't like how her story has been changed. Her story is on shelves quickly, but it hardly feels like her own anymore, and she rates the experience 3/10.

They both made $3,000. By the system of equal ratios, both authors were successful in their field; however, by their own experiences, which will reflectively impact their readers, one was much more satisfied with the final product, and therefore much more willing to go through the process again.

Let's look at authors publishing in a different way. Hillary and Michael are both authors who have chosen to self-publish their adult fiction novels.

Hillary is careful to fully edit her text. She does her research, and decides to create a print-on-demand book through Lulu, an online print-on-demand, self-publishing, and distribution platform. She knows that if she finds mistakes, she can quickly edit them. She is also in complete control of the design and cover, which she is happy for. After the book is published, Hillary dedicates a full year to online marketing, and some traveling, to promote her book. She rates the overall experience 9/10.

Michael edits several times, but is most anxious to have the book on sale. He is not a designer, and feels his masterpiece is overlooked because of the limited design elements in the cover. Months after publishing, he realizes that his publishing platform, CreateSpace, means the he can only sell through Amazon. Furthermore, his book isn't selling—not enough people are looking or clicking! He rates his success 2/10, and doesn't plan to do it again.

At the end of the year, Michael yields $3,000. By the system of equal ratios, he is as successful an author as both Sam and Rebecca, but at this point, he is frustrated and fed up with his writing career. Michael doesn't feel as successful as Sam, or even Rebecca, because time for money is not the only thing he wants. Michael wanted personal fulfillment as an author, just as Sam wanted fame, and Rebecca wanted to share a story.

At the end of the year, Hillary has earned $2,000. By the equal ratio system, she has come a mere 66 percent as far in terms of success as the other three; however, her personal experience rating is the highest of the group. In addition to a publication, Hillary sought the opportunity to be in total control of the work, and welcomed the challenges of being a one-woman publishing enterprise.

These are four hypothetical examples, which by no means explain all the variants and possibilities one may encounter in the publishing world. The difference is in the individual details. If Michael had looked more closely at his platform options, he may have found a tool that was easier to work with, or that offered him more selling platforms. If Rebecca had written a fantasy rather than a memoir, she may have felt more comfortable changing her characters. Perhaps Hillary's next book will be a historical text, and she will choose the traditional publishing route for the added eyes on editing. With her fiction still on the market, this second utilization of publication will make her a "hybrid author."

The best we have in comparing these two systems of publishing are the testimonies of such hybrid authors. Many started in traditional publishing, and were still in the publishing game when the game began to turn more towards self-publishing projects. A general agreement, gathered largely through written blog posts, states traditional publishing is a well-established system, complete with marketing teams, editing crews, designers, and deals with big name bookselling venues, as well as readers. The downside is the amount of time and rejection letters it takes before being accepted.

Self-publishing skips the disheartening rejections, and is quickly shedding the illusion of being purely vanity publications, but is much more work on the author's part, as the author is in charge of all the departmental work of a publishing house, and may have difficulty forging the connections with sellers and buyers.

Jaye Wells is a hybrid author. In a blog post for BlueInk Review, in which many types of authors were asked to complete the sentence "Self-publishing is…." Wells comments that she chose to self-publish her upcoming series of novellas because she wanted the freedom to write without traditional deadlines. "I enjoy the structure and support traditional publishing offers, but it's nice to have the ability to experiment and control scheduling with indie, as well," Wells says. Wells is a prime example of choosing one type of publishing over another to achieve a goal outside of publication and money in order to consider her endeavors successful.

Packaging the Author

Alexandria J. Allen

A recent meeting with Rachel Carter, author of the *So Close to You* time travel trilogy with HarperTeen, has inspired me to ask this question: can you achieve a successful persona in order to achieve a successful publication of a novel? Before meeting Carter, I had this romanticized notion that all books (young adult books in particular) were only created by the talented few who happened to strike gold with their million-dollar stories; however, I wouldn't say that Carter shattered my beliefs when I learned that her trilogy was the result of book packaging.

Mandy Hubbard, a writer for the website Pub(lishing) Crawl, explains that book packaging is "wherein a person or company creates marketable ideas, develops outlines or synopses, and then hires writers to write them." This definition of creating the perfect book in order to target a specific audience had me wondering about the writer. It had me questioning if it was possible to perfectly package the *author*.

I don't want to spoil anyone's favorite book, but the cash cows of book packaging have been *I Am Number Four* and the *Gossip Girl* series, just to name a couple. *I Am Number Four* became a feature-length film in 2011 and it had only been published just the year before. *Gossip Girl* hit our TV screens from 2007 – 2012 and the series publication began in 2002. With these two publications, it seems that reaching the filmmaking world was intentionally planned. I know that you have at least heard of one of these two titles, whether you knew them as films, TV series, or books. But can you tell me the name of the author of either book? I'm guessing not likely.

Book packaging makes all these efforts to get the name and summary of the book out there into the public. They want to hit their target audience with an intriguing story that they know will sell, but the name of the author isn't quite as important.

I want to raise an ethical question: is book packaging dishonest because it isn't the result of one person's single mind of imagination? Is it dishonest because these books were developed so analytically that they were literally made to *sell*? These are questions I'd like for you to consider as a reader and writer. I personally do not have much negativity towards book packaging. It is a great way to enter the publishing world, but requires some sacrifice when it comes to the rights of the creative content of the book, and the willingness to take a risk for the value of your time and talent.

So what would it be like to package the author? It would probably be much like creating a boy band. Not multiple boy singers writing a single novel but rather their essence, their alluring personalities, with their followers in tow. I've done my research, ladies and gentlemen, and the popular boy band of today, One Direction, was created through England's *The X Factor*, a talent search show. There is no sweet story to how they met, like: Harry Style's eyes met Liam Payne's eyes from across the room and they decided to make sweet, sweet music together. Nope, none of that, and yet they are in the hearts of young girls (and boys) all across the United States as well as the United Kingdom.

People have always known, even the haters, that boy bands sell, and only the haters seem to care about *why*. Watching video interviews of this quite attractive handful of young men, they come off as polite, fun, apologetic, and British (yes, this is an important point to make).

Now how can we take this trusting and attractive presentation of a boy band and translate it to an author? I'd like to refer to *A.P.E.: How to Publish a Book*, written by Guy Kawasaki and Shawn Welch. If I decided to write a novel, this would be my go-to guide and instruction manual. After reading *A.P.E.*, I found myself coming back to Chapter 23, which addresses "how to create an enchanting personal brand." Now, before I even read this chapter, I had my own personal questions about how exactly one can create such a strong online presence in order to attract the right followers and fans.

Day in and day out, I am a Tumblr junkie. I "reblog" and "like" this post and that post from the blogs that I follow, especially from the blogs that have an interesting person behind the veil of the laptop screen. Even I was falling for what Kawasaki called TLC: trustworthiness, likeability, and competence.

These are the three traits we are falling for when it comes to our favorite musicians, actors, educators, bosses, and, of course, authors. In A.P.E., Kawasaki explains that we must first build a platform, which is the "sum total of people you know and people who know you." Though Kawasaki asks us to build this type of platform, I want to touch upon the social-media platforms, such as the ever-growing YouTube.

YouTube is the bloodstream of the Internet when it comes to that talent that has yet to be tapped for cash. I myself have tried the YouTube fame route (I'll let you know what happens). It certainly isn't an easy thing to accomplish, but advice from the Internet comes in handy. According to WikiHow's "How to Make Yourself Famous on YouTube," you must first "Create a Buzz." This means being culturally relevant.

Check off competence. But cultural relevance can only take you so far. To make it in the YouTube limelight, you must create new content relentlessly. You cannot make one video, or one great short story, and expect people to kneel down at your feet and praise you for an encore. Writing is not easy and if someone has told you otherwise, just walk away. Don't waste any violent energy.

This guide to YouTube fame goes on to explain that you must also learn to connect with viewers. Check off trustworthiness. And most importantly, "Be Yourself." Check off likeability. Connecting with your viewers means actively seeking them out and also tagging your videos appropriately, along with creating an impressive-looking profile or website. Being yourself means being genuine: finding that fine line between trying too hard and not trying at all.

So here is the quick and easy way to beginning a journey of establishing the persona of the author in order to gain a following. An ethical question can be asked here as well: Is it dishonest to solely seek out an audience that you can become an opinion leader for and then *bam!* write a novel and ask them to buy it just because they like you? No.

It is not dishonest to establish yourself as a writer who has a YouTube account or an account with any other type of social media platform. Will you be as successful as John Green? The odds are not ever in your favor, my dear, but that doesn't mean you can't at least try. In a great article by the blogger Anne R. Allen, she explains that John Green does all his own marketing through "Twitter, Tumblr, and his own community forum." When he was gearing up for *The Fault in Our Stars* to come out May 2012, he even went on YouTube to read an excerpt from the book. If you want to connect with your followers and fans at the most intimate level, then I suggest you model John Green. He handles his own marketing, but this type of success isn't typical for all authors. You must first begin with nothing to create something.

It is safe to assume that social media is the way to go when trying to promote yourself as a writer. If you are well-established in an art or writing community where you live, then I suggest you take advantage of that as well. You'd be surprised to know that most people will be rooting for your success if they know they've been just the smallest bit helpful in your journey.

Packaging the *author* doesn't have to be as analytical as book packaging. No one is responsible for editing your mannerisms or opinions in order to ready you for public display. Packaging yourself as the author requires discipline with your craft and honesty with whomever you encounter through your efforts in establishing a following through an online or community presence. Having a strong, successful, and unique piece of writing is only half of being a writer. The other half is being the face for your work and being public with who you are as a great writer. Always remember: trustworthiness, likeability, and competence. These three words will take you far in your writing career.

Going Public: A Look into Online Publishers
B.H. Pitt

A writing professor of mine often said, "the last act of writing is going public." You pour hours of your life, sacrifice parts of your soul, into a piece of writing. In the end, you have a manuscript, a book waiting to be. But it's not doing anyone any good just sitting on your laptop hard drive. As a writer, you have to get your work out there and in the hands of the people.

Yet, in our modern era, that may seem harder than ever. Not because there are so few opportunities for today's writers, but because there are so many. A plethora of outlets are available for writers to get their work published: traditional print publishers are only one of them. There are so many different ways to self-publish your own work that it may make your head spin. There's also a third option: a middle ground that straddles the line between traditional and self-publishing. After putting so much work into your writing, you owe it to your piece in order to determine which outlet works best for you.

I've been working on a science-fiction novella, *Cerberus 193*, for the better part of a year now. As I've gotten toward the end of the story, I've spent a lot of time thinking about what it is I'd like to do with my finished manuscript. Very early on I decided I wanted to publish it. The question then becomes: how do I want to publish it?

Traditional print publishing seemed out of reach. Not only is it the first piece of fiction I'm looking to publish, the length—about 120 pages—doesn't necessarily afford itself to big name publishers like HarperCollins or Penguin Random House. Furthermore, I don't have an agent or the funds to hire one.

After print publishing, self-publishing seemed like it might be my best bet. Self-publishing is the burgeoning outlet for a lot of artists, writers in particular. According to a January 2013 article from *Forbes*, "as many as half" the books published in 2012 were self-published. To put that into perspective: there were about 1,000,000 books published that year.

Websites like Lulu, Amazon's CreateSpace, and AuthorHouse are specifically designed to help a writer self-publish their work. The author retains full rights to their work. Plus, many self-publishing companies offer print-on-demand, which means people have the choice whether to buy your book in physical or electronic editions.

What's more, the author makes a much higher percentage of the profits. In traditional publishing, the author gets an advance and then makes between five to ten percent of profits from book royalties, but only "once the book has sold enough to cover the publishing company's expenses," according to a *TopTenREVIEWS* article. When you self-publish, though the author pays for the initial publishing costs instead of the publisher, the author then can make up to 50 percent of the profit made on the book's sales.

Unfortunately, the production of self-published books is rather dense. "On average, [self-published books] sell less than 250 copies each," according to the January 2013 *Forbes* article. The heavy-lifting part of marketing for the books is in the hands of the authors. This means that, especially for first time authors without a following of any kind, you're going to rely mostly on how many people you can convince to buy your book via word-of-mouth and promotion on your social media.

There's also not a whole lot of structure to self-publishing. It encompasses a really wide category. Whether you publish through a place like CreateSpace or Lulu, making your book available on Amazon, or putting a PDF up on your personal website, it still falls under the umbrella of self-publishing.

There is, however, a third option: online book publishing. These companies combine elements of traditional publishers with parts of the business models from self-publishing sites to create the best of both worlds.

The author still retains full rights to their work with online publishers, and many online publishers still offer print-on-demand services. Like a traditional publisher would, an online publisher will market your book for you: "Online book publishers offer a broad selling base, whether it is through their own online bookstore or through online giants such as Amazon.com, BarnesandNoble.com, and iBookstore.com," according to another *TopTenREVIEWS* article by Noel Case.

Particularly for my first book, I'd like to have as wide of a reach as possible. I don't have a following yet and I don't trust my own ability to direct people to buy my book. There's also the potential to make more money because online publishers use a similar royalties model as self-publishing sites. So I can be making 40 – 50 percent of the profits from my work while also reaping the benefits of having my book available in places that I could never get to with self-publishing.

There's a bigger opportunity to be able to use a more traditional publisher in the future, too. Much like the paradox of getting a retail job—where no one wants to hire you if you don't have any experience, but you can't get any experience unless someone hires you—it's easier to get published if you've already been published somewhere else.

One of the largest of these online publishers is, quite appropriately, the *Digital Fiction Publishing Corp*. They publish primarily speculative fiction under their three imprints: *Digital Science Fiction, Digital Fantasy Fiction,* and *Digital Horror Fiction*. Books published under these three imprints are available on the Kindle marketplace as well as in print via print-on-demand on Amazon's main website. As of Fall 2016, they have published almost 100 novels and show no signs of slowing down. Digital Fiction Pub also produces an annual anthology of short fiction called *Quickfic*, which is available for free on their website.

Submitting my manuscript through an online publisher, such a Digital Fiction Pub, seems to make the most sense as a first-time author. It offers more reach than self-publishing would because there's a name behind it. A book that was published by an actual publisher—even an online one—is easier to find when looking online than one produced by a self-publishing service. Furthermore, it offers greater opportunities in the future. As I mentioned earlier, it's easier to publish work with a big name traditional publisher if you've already been published elsewhere.

While I put the finishing touches on my novella, and have already started planning my next several writing projects, it has paid to do some research on where I might be able to get my work so that people could read it. After all, "the last act of writing is going public." Now, I'll be informed on the best way to do that, not just for me, but the best way for the work itself.

Can an Author Self-Publish Completely by Him/Herself?

Andrea Drag

Even though the print and publication industry is experiencing impactful shifting trends—such as jobs being consolidated and full-time positions becoming term of project jobs—the self-publishing world has become a thriving alternative for authors wanting to get their book on the market and into the hands of readers. Getting from a writer's musings to the actual, tangible product of a finished book/e-book, however, is a complicated process that involves a lot of time, effort, knowledgeable resources, and skill sets that many authors might not initially consider when deciding whether to self-publish their work or not. A breakdown of these processes and tasks is needed. A completed project ready, to be distributed to the literate masses, should properly outline the answer to the ever-pondered question: Can a self-publishing author really do it all on their own? If not, how many people are needed to publish a novel?

After writing a completed book manuscript, the publication process begins. This process can be broken down into three stages: production, marketing, and distribution. For the purpose of continuity, the focus of this hypothetical publishing scenario will be a fiction novel of 70,000 words. According to the Editorial Freelancers Association, "the industry standard for a manuscript page is a firm 250 words," making this hypothetical manuscript 280 pages in length.

The production of the book is what many aspiring authors might not initially consider but is a very important component to the publishing process and could be a costly experience for self-publishers. A developmental editor, someone who makes sure the manuscript is consistent and flows without plot holes (while offering critique and revisions), is a necessity. Publishing a book without the insight from an experienced editor is as disastrous as "not testing a drug before it goes out into the marketplace," according to Miral Sattar, founder and CEO of the award-winning author services marketplace, BiblioCrunch. Hiring one of these may cost an author upwards of $2,500 (and that's on the low end of pricing, with the editor having a $45 per hour paycheck).

Another editor required for a book to get published, and taken seriously in the industry, is a copy editor whose focus is to adjust grammar consistency mistakes, correct punctuation, and catch spelling errors and missed or misused words. These can cost upwards of $800, depending on the experience of the editor and the amount of reworking a manuscript may need.

A self-publishing author could potentially avoid these costs by taking advantage of individual resources: knowing someone in the industry who is willing to do pro bono work but requires a cut of book profits, utilizing unpaid interns or students working towards a degree in writing/editing/publishing, using resources such as their college writing labs and workshops, or seeking multiple beta readers; however, these resources are either hard to come by (such as knowing someone in the industry who is willing to do anything without pay) or risk the finished quality of the novel.

An article written for www.Go-Publish-Yourself.com stresses the importance of an editor, stating that "every dollar you spend promoting an error-prone book might as well be spent in Vegas." As much as an author may think they could potentially do the job of a quality editor by him or herself, a fresh pair of eyes trained to look for inconsistencies is a valuable asset and gives the sense of professionalism to their written work. The job of a copy editor and developmental editor could potentially be consolidated into a one-person task, as long as the person in question is highly skilled and is sure to look over the manuscript with the different perspectives of both a developmental editor and copy editor. With this in mind, the publishing team of a self-published book must ultimately increase from one sole member, the author, to a team of two, the author and the editor, in order to benefit from this vital asset.

Design and layout are another skill set that the author needs to have if they are looking to publish a book on their own. They must at least have the time and dedication needed to learn the programs required for design jobs, unless they are willing to outsource to a graphic designer to complete the necessary formatting tasks. A lot of thought must go into a book's look and feel: font type and size, margins and spacing, page number location, and headings, as well as any other design elements. Will there be an imprinted logo on each page or chapter? Will the chapter titles be a different font than the rest of the novel?

Designers, if not paid a flat rate for book design, may charge design layout per page depending on the complexity of the source material. According to printing veteran Charles M. Ellertson, author of *Glossary of Typesetting Terms* and professional typesetter, $4.75 – $5.00 per page tends to be the general rate at his company, Tsengbooks. In consideration of the 280-page hypothetical manuscript, an author is looking upwards of $1,330 (with a designer charging $4.75 per page) for layout fees. A set rate for "typical design fees for the interior [of a book] with a few illustrations ranges from $600 to $850 for a complicated text."

In addition to book design formatting, the need for a graphic designer to commission the cover is arguably essential for a polished looking novel. Either having the skill set to create a professional quality cover, utilizing graphic design college interns, or using connections the author has already fostered, such as a friend who is a skilled photographer trained in InDesign, will lower the cost of these tasks. They are a necessity to the final product of the novel. "If you want to hire someone to make a custom cover design, you can expect to pay anywhere from $150 to $3,500," says Miral Sattar. Taking all this into consideration, the skills and programs required for designing a complete book from a manuscript are necessary, and it is imperative that a designer is added to the self-publishing team, making it a total of three members (in addition to the author and editor).

After production, with editing and design elements considered, a very vital portion of the publishing process comes from the marketing and PR angle. Without an audience interested in an author's work, there would be no one to distribute the book to once it is published. Book promotion involves a whole slew of skills, creative ideas, and time-dedicated projects and is an ongoing process from the start of the book's creation to the months following its publication. Creating a website or landing page for the book to sell on, with a book synopsis and author information, is essential to inform curious readers as well as to provide them with access to purchase the book in question. Being active on social media to boost a book, having a web presence, getting press releases to appropriate publications, and getting blurb reviews from credible sources all help create buzz for a novel that will soon be in publication. It is important for all these processes to be started while the book is still in the production stage so that once it is distribution-ready, there will be readers eager to get their hands on the book.

Although the author can be capable of doing all of this, they may find themselves overwhelmed enough with all the creation and production tasks—or are not particularly savvy in the online or offline promotional world—that they may want to hire someone to be in charge of marketing and PR who will not only implement promotional strategies, but also come up with creative ways to get the novel on the radar of readers everywhere. In a scenario of hiring a marketer to set up and do these tasks with, at the very least, ten hours of marketing work paid from $10 an hour (a college intern's rate) to $40 an hour (a marketing professional's rate), the low end of paid pricing for marketing will be $100 and can range upwards of $5,000 if hiring a professional book publicist, according to Miral Sattar.

Since marketing doesn't involve skills in particular digital and artistic programs or an equitable perspective separated from the source material, it does not absolutely require an additional member to the self-publishing team. A dedicated author already has the creative tendencies to write the initial manuscript and, going forth with publishing supports, a will for their book to be successful. Therefore, an author planning to self-publish can take on the role of book marketer, though the benefits of a professional are favorable.

Distribution is the final stage of publishing a novel and, with the multitude of print-on-demand options available and free or low cost online resources, it should be fairly simple for the author to get their book ready for distribution through websites like Amazon, Barnes and Noble, or Apple iBooks. The use of free digital conversion programs, such as Sigil or Calibre, can help an author get their book converted to the right digital formats for their preferred distribution method. Choosing the right self-publishing market or resource, depending on an author's end goal, is important to this stage of publication.

If a printed novel is the end goal, Lulu offers a print-on-demand option (i.e. only printing a book copy every time someone purchases the title) that makes self-publishing not only a sensible choice, but also a cost effective way for an author to get their physical book on the market. Lulu.com also offers options to distribute an e-book edition in three different online and e-reader markets including the Apple iBookstore, the Barnes and Noble Nook online store, and the Lulu e-book marketplace. For e-books to be available on Amazon's Kindle, it's required that publishers join their exclusive Amazon marketplace, separate from Lulu or other unaffiliated websites for e-book distribution, which offers a free publisher's membership. Both Lulu and Amazon take a cut of the book profits as distribution costs but do not require initial fee payments, though premium options and upgrades are available, and are user-friendly enough for a self-publishing author to follow distribution instructions. So, another member of the publishing team is not necessary with these options.

With all of these processes and tasks required to publish a book taken into consideration (production, marketing, and distribution), it is safe to say that a self-publishing author will benefit from a small team consisting of at least an editor and designer. It is a necessity. Even if the author is a jack-of-all trades-wonder-writer who is a savvy promotionalist, it's nearly impossible to expect the writer to catch every grammatical mistake or continuity error in their work and really critique their writing with the insightful candor an editor and another perspective could provide.

Professional quality formatting and design work is also something that is highly recommended to be outsourced to someone artistically trained to do so, making the smallest recommended team for a self-published book three people: the author, the editor, and the designer; however, bringing in multiple perspectives and talents to the project team for editing, designing, promotion, and distribution—either paid upfront for their services or through contracts or voluntary positions—can really benefit the author's work in the world of publication. It will create the best possible complete and refined novel of a self-publishing author's aspirations and dreams.

Section Four
The Wide World of the Web

A Funny Thing Happened When I Joined a Forum

Kara Joyce

Something fictitious, something delicious! Something poetic, something prophetic! Something for everyone, a forum for writers!

Forums have been around almost as long as the internet. They are some of the rawest forms of self-publishing, allowing anyone to publish their stories for public viewing and critique on a site for like-minded individuals. Many writing forums have popped up through the years and each has its own place in the writing community. I took a day to explore a selection of forums that were recommended to me from a variety of sources. I have weaved some into subheadings below so as not to overwhelm you, dear reader, with a huge list of links at the end of this essay. You're welcome. I've also weaved some advice into this essay so as to help you find the forum best suited to your needs as a writer.

1. Why Join a Forum?

There are many benefits to using writing forums. They open writers to an online community that allows them to interact with people who have similar writing interests and styles, and with people who enjoy the craft. On top of being able to discuss writing, many forums have sections on their sites devoted to allowing writers to post and read different types of writing and receive some editing on their pieces. Many websites also give writers access to contests on a weekly or monthly basis. All in all, forums end up being a great place to make some online connections.

WritingForums[1] is a writing forum broken down into different fields of writing-related topics. Don't know how to make your character believable for whatever reason? There's a discussion for that. Have questions about formatting? There's a discussion for that.

---

[1] Refers to www.WritingForums.com.

Want to brag to the general population that you're awesome and made it as a writer? There's definitely a discussion for that! There's also an area on WritingForums to post work with the strict idea of critique in mind. It's open to pretty much every genre you can think of and then some. The critiques are often very detailed, and you can ask for specific feedback for people to give going into the post. I perused WritingForums for a bit and found myself signing up so I could participate in some of the discussions going on. I found very few "jarhead voices." You know the type of people I'm talking about: they go on for three paragraphs about one misplaced comma and several times they use the wrong "your/you're." In general, a good chunk of the critiques and discussions are well-written and helpful.

Of course, not all forums are created equal. Being that they're free and run mainly in a question/answer format, there's bound to be a bit of a gap in the professionalism of each site. So do watch out for "jarhead voices," and avoid jumping into discussions where you see people like that.

Writing.com is one of the oldest writing forums on the Internet, founded in 2000. The setup is a bit like my old Xanga site, a site most people don't know because it hasn't been close to relevant for at least seven years. Though it's a bit outdated in appearance, there are still a decent amount of posts. It offers daily writing prompts and more contests in a month than most websites offer in a year. Some of the contests are really interesting and there are so many that it's easy to find one pertaining to a topic you'd like to write about. This is *definitely* your forum if you want a good contest.

Writing.com is probably the best place to go if your only goal is to put your work on display. They promote themselves as a way to build a portfolio. There are no open discussions, but you can request a review for your work. I joined the site to learn a bit about its inner workings. I was disappointed in the lack of open discussion, but I definitely plan to post on the site the next time I'm looking to create a portfolio since it has all the tools needed.

2. Who's on Writing Forums?

The best part of a writing forum is the diversity in the people you can interact with. This diversity brings all the voices you want to hear from about your work to your work. Oh, you're a white American man and you have a character who's a black French woman and you want to make sure your character properly portrays a woman of that description? Boom. There's probably five responses, and you might learn some French while you're at it. You're an adult writing a book for a young adult audience? Teenagers flock to writing forums like fruit flies to red wine—enjoy picking through all those responses. Yeah, I already mentioned the "jarhead voices," but those voices are pretty few and far between, unless you're on a forum dedicated to pompous people.

Figment is my personal favorite out of the forums I've joined. Though it's considered a popular writing forum for teenagers, I've found that it's one of the best places to post writing and the comments on my writing tend to be more helpful than comments on any other site. When I was first introduced to Figment, there was talk that publishers or agents or someone with power in the publishing world (I joined four years ago, I don't remember the details) would periodically read posts on the site. I don't believe that this is the case anymore; however, two years ago, the website was bought by Penguin Random House, which opened the doors to a lot of new opportunities. For example, Figment recently started hosting weekly chats where participants can write to popular writers, editors, and publishers with any questions they have about the publishing process and receive answers directly from that writer/editor/publisher.

3. What if You're a Genre Writer?

You write strictly fantasy and don't want any poetry creeping in on your territory? You write strictly poetry and you're sick of seeing fanfiction? There's a forum for you! The same way that there are different sections to a library or a bookstore, there are different sections to the internet and you're welcome to roam from section to section and choose which one is best for you. Specialized forums are more helpful in particular areas than general forums. If you're a general writer, one of the aforementioned sites is better for you. But if you tend to write a particular genre, it's best to do the digging to find a forum for your genre.

AllPoetry is a site dedicated to horror fiction. Just kidding. Naturally, it's a poetry site that allows people to post for everyone to see. The site hosts online discussion classes, which is a bit different, but the best place to go if you're having problems making that one-line break that just won't work! The website hosts monthly contests for people who participate on the site and there's a list of the top five hundred best poems available. Also, for just $35, you can be published in the annual AllPoetry Anthology and receive two copies of the publication. I don't write much poetry, so I haven't been able to explore much, but the contests are good, the layout is good, and the poetry's pretty high caliber.

FanFiction is a widely known forum for people who write fanfiction. It's famously inhabited by teenagers who like to write stories with some of the most random pairings of characters; however, its forums have good discussions. Fanfiction (though discredited by most) is a great way to hone writing skills. There's a range of abilities and subgenres in the fanfiction umbrella. I used FanFiction for a while and I was never disappointed by the feedback. One of the great things about having an account with FanFiction is that they give you statistics for your stories: where people are reading from, which of your stories gets more traffic, etc. Everything's displayed in super-easy-to-read bar graphs.

4. Which Writing Forum is Best for You?

What is it you want out of a writing forum? Do you want discussion? Are you just looking to post your writing and create an accessible online portfolio? There is a forum for you, no matter what you want out of it. If you're having any problems deciding which forum is the one for you, there are short forum discussions on Writer's Digest floating around to help you.

Lots of good posting, small room for boasting! Something for everyone: a forum for writers!

Building a Virtual Army
Jeremy Allmendinger[2]

Jeremy Allmendinger is the founder of the website Pavlov's Hair Conditioner. He is a graduate of Champlain College's Professional Writing program and is currently a digital media consultant specializing in first time authors and start-up publishers. This four-part series was written by Jeremy to explain his rise in internet popularity through the use of social media, beginning with explaining his media of choice. He shares numerous tips and tricks to gaining followers and amassing page likes on various sites including Facebook, Twitter and Instagram.

In May 2014, I was tossed into an uncertain world of possibility and failure before I could remove my mortarboard or robe. Trading a signed and stamped piece of paper for a job didn't pan out, so I did what any attention-starved millennial in my shoes would have done and took to the Internet. I've never been much for traditional employment anyway.

Before graduation, I'd spent most of my waking hours in search of online stardom. Between Pavlov's Hair Conditioner, my Facebook profile, and my Twitter account, I had a decent number of followers but still nothing to write home about. With my senior-year course load, I didn't have much time to create new content for my site, so I needed a strategy to make do with what I had. Turns out I'm really good at not creating new content.

I started my crusade on New Year's Day 2014. My stats were not very impressive. (The Facebook numbers are from my website's fan page. I didn't focus on boosting my personal profile's stats because I've been told friendship occasionally exists offline.)

---

[2]Essay was originally published on the Champlain College Publishing Initiative's blog.

Facebook	63
Twitter	41
Instagram	2
LinkedIn	158
WordPress	3,426

As of 2015, they're pleasantly inflated.

Facebook	188
Twitter	600
Instagram	212
LinkedIn	453
WordPress	7,096

By numbers alone, we're still not looking at anything too remarkable here. I've only got a few more Instagram followers than Michelangelo had. But this bump in stats was managed by spending less time online than I spend shaving. It's the five-minute abs of Internet fame.

Of course, generating new and interesting content remains the best way to gain followers short of walking on water and feeding five thousand with some bread crusts. The best advice I can give to anyone who wants online attention is to keep writing and post regularly. But schedules get full and deadlines whizz by, so thankfully there are a number of ways to supplement your website's content and still drive traffic where you want it. But first, let's talk basics.

1. Why Not WordPress?

For the past four years I've touted the benefits of WordPress. From its publicity features to its simple design and ease of use, I can't recommend another host more highly. We're not going to talk about WordPress.

You're busy. You post as much as you can but sometimes a couple days go by without your fans hearing from you. You know what's easy to use on the go? Facebook. In fact, chances are you already find yourself habitually checking from your phone or laptop. For many people it's an unconscious action. Facebook represents a switch from the old way of information gathering, in which individuals searched numerous sources for specific information. Now it's reversed. We know what source we want to read from, we just don't know what information we're looking for.

Facebook already has plenty of built-in tools and resources. Relative to most of my friends, I'm a fairly new user—I signed on in June of 2010. I was quickly hooked. What appealed to me especially was creating pages and studying the life of a post. Specifically, I watched how people interact with an update from their favorite band or TV show, from the moment it's created to its ultimate death, which I define as the last interaction before the post stops organically appearing on users' feeds.

Twitter is also a boon, but for different reasons. My Twitter account is both personal and professional. This is surprisingly common for the app, especially among people whose natural tone is similar to that of their work—think stand-up comedians and genre writers. The greatest thing about Twitter is that no one knows how to use it. The second anyone claims to have the key, the site spawns a hundred posts that behave in brand new ways. In the high school sitcom of the Internet, Twitter is the kid with the unconventional sense of humor and constantly changing wardrobe who always wants to show you the newest addition to his collection of rocks or bees or paint cans. There is no defining it and that's what makes it so perfect.

LinkedIn and Instagram are useful and often-overlooked tools even for the most unprofessional and text-oriented websites. I've gotten several publishing opportunities through my website's connection with LinkedIn, and even a few job offers. I've linked my Instagram feed to Pavlov's Hair Conditioner even though the two have nothing in common—my personal images humanize my online persona. I didn't spend too much time developing either social media channel, because neither directly connects to my website's content, but I have seen bumps in traffic after a particularly successful image post or well-connected LinkedIn share.

WordPress is a beautifully diverse group of people, but with no way to directly target individuals we need a little help to drive up that traffic count. With Facebook, Twitter, Instagram, and LinkedIn, we have much more control over who sees what and how. But before anyone can see anything, we have to build a following.

2. So You Wanna Build an Army?

Everyone hates pointless Facebook notifications. I don't care how your FarmVille is doing. I don't want to gift you pigeons in BirdBlazers. I hope your Frolic Simulator character gets an aneurysm. Similarly, sending people bushels of Facebook invites neither makes nor keeps friends. So how do I get people to like my page without bombarding them with reminders like the Allied forces in Dresden?

The answer, I found, is to bombard them slightly less. I sent everyone who might have an interest in the Pavlov's Hair Conditioner Facebook page (about 800 people) a single invite, and let them decide if they wanted to follow or not.

I also target specific pages and groups. For example, when I post a new entry in the "A Year of Ireland" series, I send a link to the still-active Facebook group of students I studied abroad with. The goal here is to keep the name "Pavlov's Hair Conditioner" somewhere in the back of people's minds. I estimate between twenty and thirty new likes came from this method, and hundreds of page views.

Twitter has been a completely different beast. At the start of my experiment, I had forty-one followers, a number which had remained stagnant for several months. In the past few weeks my followers shot up by more than two hundred. How? Well, I figured a few things out.

First off, I wasn't interacting with people nearly enough. I favorited a good number of tweets, but retweeting and especially mentions were rare at best. Similar to a Facebook like versus a comment, the former is passive and the second is active. Everyone enjoys knowing someone got a kick out of their latest post, but a personalized response—something someone took more time to write than a simple click—will always be miles above. So I simply did more of that. Several A-list musicians have since retweeted me, and I now count Ben & Jerry's as well as a fair sum of prominent bloggers among my followers.

In addition to interacting with new people, I find out who my followers follow. Twitter is great at connecting bloggers who tend to band together. The site alerts me that, say, Aussa Lorens—a popular travel writer—connected with these other notable travel writers. I'm a travel writer too, so I reach out to these newly discovered talents to see what makes them successful.

Above all, I look for people with a roughly 1:1 follower/following ratio. These users have a higher tendency to reciprocate interaction—you mention them, they'll mention you, retweet for a retweet, and so on. Most importantly, perhaps, they are most likely to follow you back.

For Instagram and LinkedIn, I took a more passive approach. Unlike Facebook, there is little expectation for a user to personally know all of their connections. As long as you have a decent number of mutuals, most users feel comfortable accepting you into their follower list. And thus do you build a wide web of potential readers. More importantly, you broaden the net for anyone looking for someone with your writing skills, which can lead to paid opportunities down the road.

3. Who Are You People?

Don't follow people you're not interested in. Chances are they're not going to be interested in you either. That said, expanding your horizons a bit—following photo bloggers even if you're not a photographer, or humor accounts from comedians you don't know—can lead to a broader, more diverse range of followers. People have many different interests.

Who follows who across these four social media platforms—Facebook, Twitter, LinkedIn, and Instagram—varies wildly. Facebook friends are usually just people you know in real life. Connections on LinkedIn benefit both parties. Each receives a potential job and a boost to their stats. In the business world, it's not uncommon to work with people you've never met. All the two have is a shared industry, mutual friends, or the same employer; however, LinkedIn retains the expectation that connections at least have something to do with each other offline.

Instagram is yet broader. Not including celebrity accounts, the majority of an Instagram user's audience consists of friends or acquaintances. At the same time, it's not unheard of to be followed by someone you've never met. The platform encourages posting about your personal life in the image-based equivalent of a Facebook status. Thus, partially out of etiquette, Instagram followers are usually people the user would be comfortable showing photos to in real life.

But not always. Instagram has become increasingly like Twitter—the most fluid of the four. I know maybe half the people I follow, and even fewer people who follow me. If an account makes me laugh, I follow it, especially if it has that golden 1:1 ratio. Twitter's openness is important. WordPress gets your name out to over 400 million people around the world, but all of that interaction is passive. Twitter, on the other hand, affords much more personal, more direct interactions. Twitter allows users to directly communicate with other users—a feature sorely lacking from WordPress. The etiquette of Twitter, especially the famous "follow for a follow," does not exist on WordPress, where many users are new not just to the host but to the Internet. For these reasons and more, I decided to focus on Twitter above all other presences.

As a result of my activity over the past few months, and in particular the last four weeks, I now have a number of big players connecting to my Twitter account, @TheAndorran. Ben & Jerry's followed me after I tweeted them my article on Free Cone Day (which they also retweeted). Their UK account followed me simply because I retweeted their Easter photo. Quite a few heavy-hitting bloggers have also signed up. Aussa Lorens I already mentioned, but I'm also followed by List of X—one of the more popular parody list accounts—as well as Idiot-Prufs, Hastywords, Edward Hotspur, and Rubber Shoes in Hell, all popular humor sites.

I'm not famous, but my star is rising.

4. Why Do Any of This in the First Place?

While Twitter has been putting along, slowly reeling in followers, my Facebook page has exploded. As of this writing I only have 191 likes, but I've left some pretty good impressions.

Facebook pages track success in hits, which they call "impressions." Beneath every post is an impression count, which represents the number of individual newsfeeds the post has appeared on. At the beginning of the year, I posted infrequently and only through a service called NetworkedBlogs, which posted automatically whenever my site had new content. Eventually I ditched the impersonal feel of NetworkedBlogs and opted to post all my own content manually. This way, I could put my own spin on everything, make it eye-catching, and hopefully attract a bit more attention than I had been. Damn if that didn't work.

Where I previously got ten or twenty impressions per post, now I regularly get over 400. I no longer post only about new content. I link to content I find funny or interesting, building relationships with other websites in the process. I also slap photos up there, and have a #PavlovThrowback feature where I highlight older Pavlov content. Whereas before I received the overwhelming majority of my traffic from WordPress, Facebook has easily taken over as my dominant referrer.

Step 1: Crowdfund.
Step 2: ???
Step 3: Profit.

Taylor Covington

In this day and age, crowdfunding can be pretty much whatever you want it to be. It can be a sob-fest for creating playgrounds for dyslexic puppies on crutches, or it can appeal to the Spock-rock minded, seeking ways to fund their new space-star-alien-navigation app; however, as far-reaching and abstract as a project may be, no one really understands what makes crowdfunding a massive success. No one really knows what sets one crowdfunding site apart from the other. No one knows if it's the theater or the film that spellbinds the audience.

Well, I'm handing you a little Zagat guide to skim. Something that you can refer to while taking a break from filming your video that advertises the lizard pajamas your wife wants to sell on Etsy, or while your new program about holistic java beans renders.

What differs one crowdfunding platform from another? Taking the top three sites from across major companies, here are my thoughts on Kickstarter, Indiegogo, and RocketHub.

At this point, you should really be asking questions, not so much about the appearance or the architecture of the site, but the community that the site promises to access. Followers lead followers. These questions should include: what do we know about the behaviors, interests, goals, and lifestyles of the people on each of these sites?

1. Kickstarter

I'll start with the famous giant, because I like to imagine myself as a modern-day David running up to Goliath and kicking him in his stupid, money-grubbing shins.

With any colossus, the brand recognition is there. Coming with it: brand equity (something I just learned in my marketing class—learning, *whoa*), which means there is a certain amount of prestige surrounding the image of Kickstarter. If your project needs a large amount of funding, Kickstarter would undoubtedly add another level of reliability, and a sense of global awareness. Plus, if a staff member "likes" your project, it will become a Staff Pick, and be featured on his or her own widely publicized front page. Unfortunately, the ratio of noticed to un-noticed is staggering. Only about twenty projects are staff-picked at one time, which leaves the other hundreds of thousands of projects left to swirl in the vast vortex of nothing that is these crowdfunding platforms.

A *New York Times* article cites these things as ways you can definitely get noticed, not only by the staff but the community at large: follow guidelines, network, and tweet and email Kickstarter employees.

One drawback is that Kickstarter does collect a five percent fee from the project—but that's only if the project is successful (meaning the goal amount is met). And here's the real pea in the princess bed: if you don't meet your goal amount, then you don't get a dime.

Overall, it's a very zany feeling that you get from this website. The background looks like the inside of a confetti cannon and the scroll option feels continuous. It's objectively smooth and most notably, the projects are creative-based. They reflect more artistic, more Etsy-powered, more cooking-with-wine-and-sushi designers. If you want to bake for orphans across the nation, or build a geo-space for West African body performers, then Kickstarter is the place for you.

2. Indiegogo

Indiegogo: the Apple to Kickstarter's Android. If Steve Jobs needed a crowdfunding site, he would go to Indiegogo.

Indiegogo is slick. Simple as that. It focuses less on supporting creative endeavors, and more on positively affecting small portions of the world. It is designed for those with business, technology, and education in mind. In this sense, where Kickstarter may raise funds for an Israeli cookbook, Indiegogo creates portable heating lamps for explorers in the Patagonia. Again, there is no set-up fee or processing period. Furthermore, Indiegogo has about 24 different categories of projects, opposed to Kickstarter's 15. But the biggest glaring opposition to Kickstarter is that if you do not meet your goal, you still get to keep that money.

However, there are no staff picks. Those featured on the main page are "trending" and reach that cover status through raising the highest amount of money. Indiegogo also takes the five percent of the total money raised, whether or not you meet your goal. Despite having more options to pay (PayPal, credit card, wire transfer), there are still transaction fees—which vary on the type of payment made.

Indiegogo has an interesting dynamic. It is, in my opinion, more professionally sound. It's not that I doubt the reliability of Kickstarter, but the authenticity presented by the overall design, organization, and flow of Indiegogo is relayed to their projects. If I were to donate money to any number of projects, I know it would go to a socially just cause. That being said, as I've already stated, Kickstarter is Kickstarter. Everyone talks about it, knows about it, and therefore, may be more inclined to donate because of the brand equity.

From what I've seen, Kickstarter is obsessed with the human element.

It celebrates the wacky and the weird and ceremoniously places it on a glittering pedestal. If some stay-at-home-mom in Idaho is truly passionate about her fleece-made *Harry Potter* characters, then Kickstarter will bow down and worship it. And here comes the dichotomy: do we, as potential donators, value a human story or human-saving technology more? Obviously, that may vary for each individual, but that is something to consider when choosing where to place your own project.

3. RocketHub

Now let's take a wide left turn into oncoming traffic—in a safe, inflatable ball that lets us gently hover over all the turmoil.

In fairness to the subject as a whole, I have spent little time interacting with RocketHub in comparison to the previous two sites. But, what's interesting to note is that this rarely comes up in conversation—despite being on multiple lists as effective crowdsourcing platforms. As designers, is it important for our projects to be spread word-of-mouth, or via the Internet?

Interestingly enough, RocketHub is attempting to quite literally jettison their way into popular media. Recently, they've teamed up with A&E (yes, the TV channel, famous for their airings of Duck Dynasty) to spotlight certain projects. This means a whole crew of cameras, interviewers, and heat-exhaustion-inducing lights could come to you and broadcast your kitten mittens to the world. They encourage industry news: what's happening in your project's field, what has changed, what might change, how are your competitors dealing with the problems you are facing?

The most immediate, and startling, difference between the previous two and RocketHub is the perceived community. Since I have not used RocketHub before, I cannot speak adequately to this "community," but it seems that their goal as a crowdfunding platform is to get the message out there, through all means of social media, previous investors, and future leaders.

Financially speaking, there are no start-up fees and you get to keep any money earned (just like Indiegogo). As someone who likes to know exactly what they're going in to, RocketHub blasts away Indiegogo and Kickstarter with their very in-depth, detailed Q&A page. If you've got a question, there's an answer there somewhere.

If the project should succeed, they take a four percent commission fee *and* a four percent credit card handling fee. If the project doesn't succeed, there's an eight percent commission and four percent credit card handling fee. Another drawback is the flow of the website itself. It feels almost like a Tumblr page: continuous scroll-function with slowly loading graphics. The site as a whole has a much more buttoned-up feeling. With the text in an outdated font, and the colors as a whole leaving much to be desired, RocketHub appears to be a website set up by your uncle who works in the government. It carefully straddles the TED Talks image against Jeff Daniel's face in the Newsroom. If your project aims to be more standard and rhetoric, then there is no shame in using this site.

For all its lack of frills, RocketHub absolutely gets the job done.

4. Summary

It's summer time and we're sitting out at your grandmother's farm in upstate New York. The sun has set into a purple bloom in the sky, and it's time to choose a movie.

If your project is *Sweet Home Alabama* or *Waitress* (with Nathan Fillion), then go with Kickstarter. If your project is *Being John Malkovich* or *Eternal Sunshine of the Spotless Mind,* then go with Indiegogo. If your project is *The West Wing* or the documentary *Helvetica*, then go with RocketHub.

Now let's see that movie magic.

The Future of Blogging and the Broken Internet Sales Model

Zack Miller

It's estimated that 6.7 million people blog on blogging sites, 12 million people blog on social media, and that 77 percent of Internet users read blogs. All of these numbers are trending upward, but what does that mean for the long-term staying power of blogs versus traditional journalism? Right now, the future is in user-created content.

Sometimes, I feel like we've heard everything there is to say about blogs, both positive and negative. It's either "Everyone has a blog nowadays, and most of the bloggers can't even write," or it's "Everyone should have a blog. If you don't, you're not hip," or whatever the kids say these days. Independent bloggers have a love/hate relationship with their audiences without the guise of a large media conglomerate to hide behind.

I've managed my own blog for almost a year and a half, interviewing artists big and small, controversial and non. What I've discovered is that the very power I use in order to post my work is the same power @ilykebutts69 uses to tweet at me and tell me that 1) I suck, or 2) the artist I interviewed sucks and doesn't deserve press.

That's the beauty of the Internet. It gives the loudest can room to rattle, and I include myself in that. If it's so volatile, so hateful, so full of people with poor grammar and hashtags that make no sense, how is it that blogging and user-generated content are the media giants of now and of the future? For a few reasons:

1. Numbers Never Lie

Twitter, Tumblr, Wordpress, and all of the other blogging sites that popped up in the time it took me to type this sentence, are showing huge numbers and continuing to grow. Facebook is the social media tool that seems to be going out of style. Maybe the other ones I listed eventually will, too. That's the nature of products. It's the same reason I don't own a Members Only jacket or Hammer Pants. But guess what? People still wear pants. Blogging is the new pants. Regardless of how they change, they aren't going away anytime soon.

2. Creativity Is Innate

User-generated content might be the newest wave of online content, but creativity has been around since the first caveman scratched a picture of a mammoth onto a rock and showed it to his friend. The idea that anyone with a basic knowledge of the Internet can login and create something that would have been seen as impossible a few years ago is an insane draw. Don't underestimate how much satisfaction people get out of doing whatever they want.

3. Impatience and Instant Gratification

The reason I started my blog is to create what I wanted to see on the Internet. I am not special. There are millions of other people that are dissatisfied with what they see and will go on to create exactly what they want. Why? Because they want it. Newspapers can't give them that. Magazines can't give them that. Maybe scrapbooking can if you're really good at it? My point is: people want what they want, and now they can do it. That's not going away anytime soon. In fact, that attitude is probably growing.

What does this mean for traditional journalists? I don't think it means anything, except the general rule to not believe everything you read on the Internet. Traditional outlets have lots of editors and fact-checkers, things that not every blogger has or possibly even wants. But at the core, a journalist and a blogger come from the same spirit—a journalist might just have more patience; however, storytelling, sharing, and community exist in both. There is no blogging vs. journalism.

Now that we've established that the writing hasn't changed, we need to look at what has drastically changed: the sales model. Unfortunately, the sales model for Internet property is already broken. Ads are not enough in the first place and people don't want them. But, most people also don't want to go through a pay-wall either. There is a sense of entitlement that exists in Internet property that rarely exists in the physical world. In essence, it's not stealing if I can't hold it, touch it, or physically take it from your cold dead hands.

The majority of frequent Internet users want free stuff. We all do, really. But the problem with "free" is that when it's used too often, it becomes unappreciated and feeds the beast that is point number three. Suddenly, everyone will want everything for free, and if they can't have it that way, they won't want it at all.

In one of my recent interviews for my blog, I talked with rapper Qali Stacks from San Diego. While discussing his music, the conversation turned to release methods. Would it be on iTunes or other paid music platforms? Or would he release it for free on a website like Datpiff? Considering that many rappers start out by giving things out for free to establish an immediate fan base, his response surprised me. He told me that although he may do a few special giveaways, he would never completely give away his work for free.

"First off, I'm trying to establish brand. Why would I give it away to a site like Datpiff where they use it to build their own brand?" asked Stacks. "If I give it away for free, I'm not giving it any value. How can I expect other people to value my craft if I don't value it enough to charge for it?"

I agree with him 100 percent and believe the same rules can exist for blogging. When a writer spends hours crafting something to be pleasurable for the reader, why can't there be compensation? If you love your product, you should be able to charge for it.

That's exactly where I think user-generated content is heading. As more and more of it hits the Internet, the market will need to adapt, not in a journalistic sense, but in its sales model. Blogging and journalism aren't going anywhere, but maybe it's worth a few bucks to keep around, just in case.

Acknowledgements

I would like to thank the people who helped make this project possible: Kim MacQueen, who steered the ship in the right direction; all the insightful authors who shared their wisdom with us; and the amazing Champlain College Publishing Initiative's staff who made it into a reality. We couldn't have done it without you.